The Bullied Anthology:

Stories of Success

Reading Harbor Publishing

Lansdale, PA

First Edition: 2015

Also by Reading Harbor:

Seeking Human Kindness

Reading Harbor

Lansdale, PA 19446

Visit our website at www.readingharbor.com

First Edition: June 2015

Printed in the United States of America

For the misfits

Just when the caterpillar thought the world
was over, it became a butterfly. . . —Proverb

Contents

Prologue 9

Preventing Peer Victimization 13

The Ultimate Revenge 24

Part I: Confidence 35

Breaking the Cycle of Bullying 36

A Taste of Bullying 39

Getting Free 44

No Safe Haven 50

Growing from the Inside 55

To Be Like the Cool Kids 62

Life Can Be Hard for an Introvert 66

Part II: Education 74

The Turning Point   60

On Bullying 80

From Victim to Expert 85

Part III: Friendship 75

Bringing Down the Bullies 97

Alone.. 102

Part IV: Helping Others.. 84

The Wallflower 110

Training Bras and Torture 116

Part V: Outside Help.. 92

On the Roadside 121

Danny 123

You're Cool.. 127

How I Overcame Being Bullied............................. 130

Stand Up Even If You Are Alone 134

Part VI: Perseverance.. 108

Small-Town Kid 140

From Victim to Victor... 145

Never Give Up.. 153

Survival Mode.. 160

Part VII: Yourself... 128

The Swan 167

Like Oil and Vinegar 170

Be Your Own Success Story.......................................174

Apprehension 181

Mean Girls..184

Acknowledgments 188

Prologue

"People who love themselves don't hurt other people."

—Dan Pearce, Author of *The Real Dad Rules*

This book is dedicated to those who are facing tough odds or stacked challenges. It is for those who have found themselves on the opposite side of the crowd. For the misfits. The outcasts. The ones who didn't quite fit in. It's for those who were picked on, tormented, teased, or harassed—just for being different. This book is a reminder that a rock under pressure can turn into a diamond. Being bullied is not a death sentence if you don't let it be. Being bullied is unpleasant. It is terrible. It is wrong. A moral and social evil. And it is entirely the fault of the one who chooses to bully and those who stand by and watch—not the victim.

Bullying is an epidemic.[1] Almost everyone will experience torment at some point in their life. Bullying occurs when anyone uses superior strength or influence to intimidate you, to force you to do anything you do not want to do, or to hurt you again and again in an unreasonable manner.[2] It happens in schools, homes, and even workplaces.[3] It happens to men and women. It happens to both old and young. Children and adults alike can be perpetrators or victims of bullying.[4] Anyone can be targeted. Yet despite its prevalence, it is rarely discussed.

Bullying is an uncomfortable topic.[5] It involves talking about unpleasant experiences. It involves negative emotions, such as pain and embarrassment. When confronted, perpetrators often forget or justify their misconduct. On the other hand, victims rarely ever forget. Victims often feel a deep sense of shame. Some question whether they did something to "deserve" being bullied and even blame themselves. A number of bullying victims take drastic action upon themselves and never recover. But others use their horrific experience and turn it into something else entirely. Instead of letting the pain destroy them, they let it mold them and strengthen them, just as iron can be forged into steel.

Survivors take the negativity that they were fed and, instead of letting it pull them down, they rise above it. They learn from it and grow from it. They use their experience as fuel to light their inner fire, to motivate them toward their goals. They become smarter, wiser, and kinder—pushing themselves beyond ordinary boundaries. They use their misfortune to propel them forward into a future brimming with success and happiness. These are their stories.

For those who are looking for inspiration in moments of trial, these stories capture what others have done to survive personal struggle. Everyone has some battle to be fought. What these stories show is that even if something horrible happens to you, there is more than one way to survive and even thrive. Each of these former "victims" found a way to overcome bullying, harassment, torment, and abuse to achieve their dreams and become wildly successful.

They wanted to share their stories in order to help others who have faced or are facing the same situation. You are not alone. What happened to you happens to others. Overcoming bullying is something that can make you even stronger and even greater. Remember, if you choose not to bully, you are already better than the one who chooses the destructive path.

—Grace Chen

Founder of Reading Harbor

References

1. "Bullying Statistics." Pacer's National Bullying Prevention Center. http://www.pacer.org/bullying/about/media-kit/stats.asp Retrieved Apr 19, 2015.

2. Volk, Anthony A., Andrew V. Dane, Zopito A. Marini. "What is Bullying? A theoretical redefinition." *Developmental Review*. Volume 34. Issue 4. December 2014. Pages 327–343. Retrieved Oct 14, 2014.

3. Loerbroks, Adrian, Matthais Weigl, Jian Li, Jurgen Glaser, Christiane Degen, Peter Angerer. "Workplace bullying and depressive symptoms: A prospective study among junior physicians in Germany." *Journal of Psychosomatic Research*. Volume 78. Issue 2. February 2015. Pages 168 172.

4. Nielsen, Morten B., Tone Tangen, Thormod Idsoe, Stig Berg Mattheisen, Nils Mageroy. "Post-traumatic stress disorder as a consequence of bullying at work and at school. A literature

review and meta-analysis." *Aggression and Violent Behavior.* Volume 21. March–April 2015. Pages 17–24.

5. Horner, Stacy, Yvonne Asher, and Gary D. Fireman. "The impact and response to electronic bullying and traditional bullying amongst adolescents." *Computers in Human Behavior.* Volume 49. August 2015. Pages 288–295. Retrieved Mar 21, 2015.

Preventing Peer Victimization

By David A. Machine, MA, Psychotherapist,

Adjunct Instructor in Psychology and Criminology

Introduction

Victimization can occur in many contexts, including domestic violence, child maltreatment, assault, muggings, sexually based offenses, and bullying. This article will focus on victimization through bullying, also known as peer abuse, and how to respond. This article is written for a wide audience; parents, educators, and school administrators, as well as teens, may find the information useful. It may also help those who have endured bullying to gain some perspective.

Defining Victimization

When you are a victim, you have been targeted for mistreatment or abuse by others—in the case of bullying, your peers. Your peers are people in about your own age group with whom you associate regularly. Being a victim implies that you have not been a deliberate and active participant in the abuse but rather an unwilling participant. If a seventh grader goes up to another seventh grader and spews insults about his or her mother and then gets hit, the person doing the insulting is not a victim—he or she is an active participant in the process of violence. Two teens who have a problem with each other and agree to fight are also active participants. Some of this is alpha-male posturing, which is common among young men. Typically, a few punches are thrown, they grab each other and roll around on the ground, and the winner has established his dominance. Often, little actual damage is done. In contrast, victims are generally smaller, weaker kids who are less sure of themselves, sensitive, shy, socially awkward, or naive, or they have a different appearance or qualities from the norm—too tall, too short, too fat, too skinny, too dumb, too smart, too *whatever*. For kids like this, being bullied is not schoolyard alpha-posturing, or a rite of passage, or just kids fooling around. It is always anxiety provoking, terrifying at times, and humiliating, and it can result in injury as well as long-term problems.

The Cost of Bullying

Bullying is often referred to as a rite of passage, kids being kids, kids playing around. It can be those things, but it can also be abusive, physically injurious, and psychologically damaging. Some kids who are bullied are driven to suicide. Bullied kids are between two and nine times more likely to attempt suicide than kids who are not bullied.[1] Others can develop PTSD (post-traumatic stress disorder), other anxiety disorders, depression, eating disorders, and substance abuse problems. Others may become weary enough of the abuse and angry enough that they go to the opposite extreme and switch from being a victim to being an aggressor. As adults, they may engage in criminal behavior or may have multiple psychological problems that carry over into adulthood.

How to Respond

The bullies are probably not going to change, except to get worse. My experience has led me to believe that schools typically do very little to protect bullied students. Many schools have anti-bullying programs, but their effectiveness is questionable. A recent study of seven thousand students from across the United States indicated that active anti-bullying programs actually make bullying worse for kids.[2] Therefore, you have to take responsibility for your own safety.

- Don't look like a victim.

    Carry yourself with confidence. Don't slouch—stand up straight. Keep your head up and be aware of your surroundings. Since predators look for submissive, uncertain behaviors, carrying yourself with confidence can reduce your chance of being victimized.[3] No texting and walking, or daydreaming. Never look hesitant or lost, even if you are.[4]

    Make good eye contact, but do not glare or stare at others.

    Dress neatly and be clean. People who have a squared-away appearance—neat, orderly, and symmetrical— tend to project self-confidence and self-valuing. This does not mean expensive, designer-label clothing or tough-guy clothes. Being squared away is the opposite of looking sloppy, disheveled, or disorganized. Don't try to dress like a gangsta if you are not. You will just amuse or upset the real ones.

    Get fit. I cannot emphasize this enough. Bullies look for weakness to exploit.[3] Getting fit does not necessarily mean bodybuilding and developing mass. This may be a goal if you are extremely underweight, but getting fit means developing, caring for, and valuing your body, for real. Getting fit will make you feel different about yourself, and you will carry yourself differently. A study of how convicts select victims indicated that they unconsciously look for people who walk awkwardly, which they interpret as a sign of being unfit or uncoordinated.[5, 3] When you get fit, other people will notice and will respond to you with more respect. This is what I mean when I say it will be for real. It will come from deep inside you—it will not be something you are faking. Running, biking, swimming, calisthenics, weight training; eating right; getting enough sleep and rest; and not abusing your body with cigarettes, drugs, or alcohol are all part of fitness. As a teen, your body is growing and developing. Make fitness a lifelong habit and maximize your strength, agility, endurance, and coordination.

- Don't talk like a victim.

    Look people in the eye when you speak to them.

    Be polite and respectful, but firm.

    Project your voice but don't bark. Speak in a clear, strong voice. You also don't have to insert profanity into every sentence. Doing that just makes you sound as though you are trying to act tough.

Don't hesitate or murmur when you speak—speak decisively but not arrogantly.

- Don't act like a victim.

A potential target cannot show any fear; it will invite aggression.[6] A potential target can't display too much emotion. I know this contradicts so much of modern psychology. Contemporary psychology spends a great deal of time extolling the value of being in touch with your emotions and not holding in emotions, as suppression of emotions can lead to psychological harm. That is theory. Here is reality: a kid who cries easily, overreacts emotionally to minor scrapes or injuries, whines, shows fear, or becomes impotently enraged will be a source of great amusement for bullies. A young person being bullied can acknowledge any feelings to him- or herself as well as to trusted adults or peers, and cry later if he or she needs to, but not in front of bullies.

Get some allies. Making friends helps bullied kids learn social skills and be less socially awkward. Bullies are less likely to target groups of friends or more popular kids.[7]

Tell an adult? This is a tough one. Many kids will be very resistant to getting adults involved, as this will get them a reputation as a tattler, rat, or snitch. It may invite even more abuse. It sends the message that: 1) the victim can't stand up for him— or herself and needs adults; 2) the victim will get others involved to protect him or her.[6] This is complicated, as there are pros and cons. However, if the parents or school authorities are told and the response is ineffective, it will be even more demoralizing for the bullied child.

Should you fight? In my opinion, and that of many other experts in the field of violence, no. Fighting means you have become a participant in the violence. But you can use force to defend yourself. There is a big difference. Defining the difference further is beyond the scope of this article and entails many complexities; however, see the Resources section at the end of the article for further information that can get you started.

- Don't think like a victim.
  - o Do you value yourself enough to protect yourself? If not, most of the bullies' work is already done for them. Bullies target kids who are already demoralized and beaten inside. Many victims don't fight back because they don't think they have the right to protect themselves. They have been conditioned to be passive and helpless. Start questioning this way of thinking.

Hot Zones

The similar dynamics between a middle school and a maximum security prison are remarkable. In school, bullying will most likely take place when there is no adult supervision and at transitional times when large numbers of students are moving from one place to another. Ironically, a similar dynamic is seen in prisons—violence is most likely to occur in the prison yard or the chow hall, where large numbers of inmates are congregating, or when inmates are moved between locations like the yard, showers, or chow hall. In both middle schools and prisons, the weak are singled out and victimized, or vengeance for a perceived slight is carried out. To stay safer, you must be aware of your surroundings and analyze your environment. Identify the times and places where bullying is most likely to occur.

The most likely places and times are:

- Before school
- Between classes
- Gym
- Lunch
- After school
- Outside of school

A possible strategy for avoiding bullying is to get permission from the school to take different routes between classes so your whereabouts are less predictable and you're therefore less vulnerable.[4] Looking for alternate routes to and from school, if you are on foot, or getting a ride home from adults may also cut down on bullying exposure. Gym is a hard time for targets of bullying. Your physical skills are tested, and if you don't perform well you will be marked as weak and an easy target. Once again, develop a high degree of physical fitness. It will help.[3] (See the Resources section at the end of this chapter for further information on fitness.) Lunch hour is the social hour, where hierarchies of friendships and connections are made and social skills are practiced. Social ineptitude will make a shy, timid teen a target.

Are You in a Position to Help?

If you are a bigger kid reading this—maybe an athlete or one of the popular kids—what do you do when you see smaller, weaker kids getting bullied? Nothing? Do you watch and laugh? Join in? Consider doing something to protect the smaller kids who are less capable of defending themselves. I am not suggesting beating up the bullies, no matter how much they have worked to earn it. That will just backfire and get you in trouble. There are other ways. You could intervene and escort the weaker kid away. Your presence may be enough to discourage the bullies. I remember a scene from high school when I was a freshman. Two freshmen were going to fight. A bunch of us were gathered around to watch them. A senior on the football team came over and calmly asked what we were doing. He suggested to the two contestants that fighting would be a bad idea and that they should just go home. They wisely and quietly took his advice and went their separate ways. No damage done.

Some Final Thoughts for Targets of Bullies

Bullies want to make you feel as though you are helpless. They want to keep you weak so they can use you for their own sick, twisted purposes. They want to hurt and humiliate you so they can feel better about themselves. That is all they have. They are pretty pathetic. You do not have to be their target. Make yourself stronger—in your mind, body, and spirit—and you can become safer.

References

1. Bullying Statistics. Bullying and Suicide. *Bullying Statistics.* Retrieved April 27, 2015 from http://www.bullyingstatistics.org/content/bullying-and-suicide.html.

2. Trowbridge, A. Are Anti-bullying Efforts Making It Worse? *CBS News.* 2013. Retrieved April 27, 2015 from http://www.cbsnews.com/news/are-anti-bullying-efforts-making-it-worse.3. LaHaie, R. Why Is Everybody Always Picking On Me? Short Circuiting theVictim Selection Process. *Protective Strategies.* 2011. Retrieved April 26, 2015, from http://www.protectivestrategies.com/victim-selection.html.

4. Shankman, P. How to Avoid Being a Victim, Anywhere, Any Time. 2012. Retrieved April 26, 2015, from http://shankman.com/how-to-avoid-being-a-victim-anywhere-any-time.

5. Hustmyre, C., J. Dixit. Marked for Mayhem. *Popular Psychology.* 2009. Retrieved April 26, 2015, from https://www.psychologytoday.com/articles/200812/marked-mayhem.6. Macyoung, M., D. G. Macyoung. Bullies, Not Backing

Down and Other Macho BS. *No Nonsense Self-Defense*. 2008. Retrieved April 26, 2015, from http://www.nononsenseselfdefense.com/bullies.htm.

7. Bryner, J. Bullies Pick on Unpopular Kids, Study Finds. *Live Science*. 2010. Retrieved April 26, 2015, from http://www.livescience.com/8155-bullies-pick-unpopular-kids-study-finds.html

8. United States Krav Maga. Do You Look Like a Victim? *United States Krav Maga's blog*. 2010. Retrieved April 26, 2015, from https://unitedstateskravmaga.wordpress.com/2011/02/12/do-you-look-like-a-victim.

Resources for Further Reading

Debecker, Gavin. *The Gift of Fear*. Dell: NY, 1997.

Kane, L., K. Wilder *Little Black Book of Violence*. YMMA: Wolfsboro, NH, 2010.

Keegan, P. We Won't Let Him Hurt You: Everlasting Fitness Through the Painless Socratic Method, with Help from Our Favorite Answer Man. *Outside.com*. 1998. Retrieved April 27, 2015 from http://www.outsideonline.com/1838101/we-wont-let-him-hurt-you.

Macyoung, M. *Violence, Blunders and Fractured Jaws: Advanced Awareness Techniques and Street Etiquette*. Paladin Press: Boulder, CO, 1992.

Macyoung, M., D. G. Macyoung. *No Nonsense Self-Defense.com*

Miller, R. *Meditations on Violence.* YMMA: Boston, 2008.

Scott, P. The Shape of Your Life. *Outside.com.* 2015. Retrieved April 27, 2015 from http://www.outsideonline.com/1966536/shape-your-life.

About the Author

David A. Machine is a college instructor, psychotherapist, and avid amateur athlete. He helps victims of violent crime to cope and adjust, and works to prevent violence through an anger management program with violent offenders. He loves to run, lift weights, read, cook, take photos, learn, share ideas with others, and sometimes just sit and enjoy the silence and solitude. He has had personal experience with being bullied.

The Ultimate Revenge

"The best revenge is massive success."
—Frank Sinatra, Entertainer

Celebrity

As anyone who owns a TV can attest to, celebrities are lauded and venerated as modern-day heroes. Their footprints are captured in the stone walkways of buildings. Their photographs and autographs are treasured and traded as valuable keepsakes and memorabilia. They are considered the most beautiful, the most talented, and the brightest of all entities—in short, stars. Adored by the public and envied by millions who would love to be in their place, they command legions of followers and hefty paychecks for the smallest of public appearances. But as much as they are loved today, many did not always fit in. Growing up, many encountered difficulties, and some of them fell victim to bullying before later achieving outrageous success.

The stark contrast of who they are today and where they came from is an interesting juxtaposition. What they have to say about their past is enlightening. For the thoughtful observer, some lessons can be learned. Celebrities, like each of us, are human. Humans are capable of extraordinary achievement. The path you start on may lead you to an incredible journey. Even if you are mistreated and have humble beginnings, the future can be dramatically different from your current experience.

Quotes

"I was bullied so badly, my dad used to have to walk me into school so I didn't get attacked. I'd eat lunch in the nurses' office so I didn't have to sit with the other girls. Apart from my being mixed race, my parents didn't have money so I never had the cute clothes or the cool backpack."

—Jessica Alba, *Daily Mirror*

"Growing up, I did not feel safe. Feeling powerless is the worst feeling in the world. I turned to singing as an outlet. The pain at home is where my love for music came from. . . . I have definitely experienced forms of bullying, and that's why it's so important for me to write songs like 'Beautiful' and 'Fighter.'"

—Christina Aguilera, *E!*

"I took a beating from several boys for years. They put me through hell, punching and kicking me all the time."

—Christian Bale, *Contact Music*

"People called me Olive Oyl, Lightbulb Head and Fivehead, because my forehead was so big."

—Tyra Banks, *GQ*

"They [bullies] were literally picking things up out of the puddles and throwing them at me, and I just stood there on my own. No one was with me. I didn't have any friends. People would push me around, say they were going to beat me up after school, chase me. It was miserable, my whole schooling, miserable. I tried to be friends with people, but I didn't fit in. So I kept to myself."

—Victoria Beckham, *Elle Magazine.*

"I'd come back [to school] from Europe, and I looked like a clown compared to the cool way the other students looked and dressed. So I got my ass whooped a little bit. . . . Kids are mean, and the sad thing is I can still remember the first and last names of every one of those kids who were mean to me!"

—Sandra Bullock, *Huffington Post*

"I was bullied quite a lot when I was growing up in my Peking Opera School. I allowed myself to be bullied because I was scared and didn't know how to defend myself. I was bullied until I prevented a new student from being bullied. By standing up for him, I learned to stand up for myself."

—Jackie Chan, *3 News*

"[At a dance in junior high, an older student] slugged me in the jaw as hard as he could. I just stood my ground and stared at him. . . . I had learned that I could take a hit and there's more than one way to stand against aggression."

—Former President Bill Clinton, *My Life*

"I was very tiny. . . . I spent most of my time stuffed into lockers. Thank God for cell phones, or I'd still be in there."

—Chris Coffer, New Yorker Festival

"So many times the big bully comes up, pushes me. Your heart's pounding, you sweat, and you feel like you are going to vomit. I'm not the biggest guy; I've never liked hitting someone, but I know if I don't hit that guy hard, he's going to pick on me all year. I go, 'You better fight.' I just laid it down. I don't like bullies."

—Tom Cruise, *Parade Magazine*

"The girls took it beyond normal bullying. These were big, tough girls, I was scrawny and short. They were fully capable of doing me bodily harm. They shoved in [the school bathroom]. I was trapped. I banged on the door until my fists hurt. Nobody came. I spent what felt like an hour in there, waiting for someone to rescue me, wondering how my life had gotten so messed up."

—Miley Cyrus, *Miles to Go*

"Growing up, a lot of the girls in my school started developing quickly. My mom has a very pronounced bust line and I was a late bloomer. One of my worst memories was getting dressed up for a school activity and having the girls pick on me because I was flat chested. I was very much a tomboy for a long time."

—Rosario Dawson, *PBS Kids*

"I got beat up all the time in high school . . . I was the underdog. All of my angst comes from that [time] in my life."

—Fred Durst, *E! News*

"Usually the bullies are the most insecure. I was bullied and it's hard; you feel like high school's never going to be over. It's four years of your life and you just have to remember the person picking on you has their own problems and their own issues. And you're going to be OK."

—Megan Fox, *E! News*

"I had a very funny-looking face when I was little. I had like big eyes, big lips, big ears. But when I was little I was constantly being made fun of for having big eyes and that was awful. I used to come home crying, 'Why do I have big eyes?' And my parents were like, 'You're crazy!' I've learned it wasn't a bad thing to be picked on because when you're little, it seems awful, like it's the end of the world. I grew into my face."

—Mila Kunis, *OK! Magazine*

"I didn't fit in at high school. I wanted to be like Boy George and I felt like a freak."

—Lady Gaga, *Ellen*

"I had the worst high school experience ever. I went to a very mean school and was bullied like crazy. . . . If I could go back and tell my 14-year-old-self anything, it would be, 'Don't worry. You're going to be doing exactly what you want to be doing, and those people who are assholes now are still going to be assholes in 20 years. So let it go!'"

"I was bullied as a young boy. They would tie my ankles up with a very rough rope and hang me in a tree upside down, spit on me and call me names, even hold a gun to my head. I didn't tell anybody— my parents or teachers or friends or sisters. I know now that the worst thing you can do is suffer in silence."

—Derek Hough, *GLSEN Gala*

"I changed schools a lot when I was in elementary school because some girls were mean. They were less mean in middle school because I was doing all right, although this one girl gave me invitations to hand out to her birthday party that I wasn't invited to. . . . Don't worry about bitches—that could be a good motto, because you come across people like that throughout your life."

—Jennifer Lawrence, *Sun Magazine*

"I had a really tough time when I was in middle school. People would write 'hate petitions' [about me] and send them around to be signed. They'd have CD-bashing parties of my demos. They'd come to my house, stand across the street and yell things. It was a very emotional time for me, and all I wanted to do was get away."

—Demi Lovato, *People Magazine*

"The boys in my school would make fun of me. [They would call me] hairy monster. . . . And then going to high school, I saw how the popular girls had to behave to get the boys. I knew I couldn't fit into that. So I decided I would do the opposite. I refused to wear makeup [or] to have a hairstyle. . . . Straight men did not find me attractive. I think they were scared of me because I was different."

—Madonna, *Harper's Bazaar*

"I became a victim of bullying. I was a gawky, skinny girl with big teeth and that made me an easy target. I had two bullies and they tortured me all through junior high school."

—Eva Mendes, *Daily Mail*

"I was an overweight kid, and I went through a period where . . . they were making cow sounds at me when I walked down the hallway and just humiliating me. That's when I got into martial arts and no one ever picked on me again."

—Jillian Michaels, *Health Magazine*

"It would certainly be accurate to say that I did not have a good childhood. It was not absent of good, but it was not a happy childhood. It was like misery."

—Elon Musk, *Sunday Times*

"I have to say that with big ears and the name that I have, I wasn't immune [to being bullied]. I didn't emerge unscathed. As adults, we all remember what it was like to see kids picked on in the hallways or in the school yard. Bullying isn't the problem that makes headlines every day. But every day, it touches the lives of young people all across the country."

—President Barack Obama, White House Conference on Bullying

"It's kind of crazy. When I do go up around where I used to live [in Baltimore], you still see the same people who were picking on me. They're still around, busing tables or whatever, probably still acting the same way. They'll try to talk to me and I'm thinking, 'Yeah, why are [you] talking to me now? You were picking on me back then.'"

—Michael Phelps, *Yahoo Sports*

"We lived in Bed-Stuy, one of the most famous ghettos in the world. My mother and father wanted me to go to a better school, so I was bused to this poor, white neighborhood. . . . I was the only black boy in my grade for most of the time. I was a little guy, too, a skinny runt. . . . Put the most successful men and women in the world in one room, and ask them to put their hands up to see which ones were bullied. Most of 'em! [Bullying was] the defining moment of my life. . . . It made me who I am." –

—Chris Rock, *BET*

"Kids back home in Texas, who I thought were my friends, were saying things behind my back. They said that I would never make it because I wasn't talented or pretty enough to be on TV. They also said I wasn't funny and would constantly ask me why I was even trying. I won't lie, it hurt. Bad. Why would my 'friends' turn against me?”

—Raini Rodriguez, *J-14 Teen Magazine*

“I was wearing an old Salvation Army shop boy’s suit. As I went to the bathroom, I heard people saying, ‘Hey, faggot.’ They slammed my head into a locker. I fell to the ground and they started to kick the shit out of me. I had to have stitches. The school kicked me out, not the bullies. Years later, I went to a coffee shop and I ran into one of the girls who kicked me, and she said, ‘Winona, Winona, can I have your autograph?’ And I said, ‘Do you remember me? Remember in seventh grade you beat up that kid?’ And she said, ‘Kind of.’ And I said, ‘That was me. Go f*** yourself.’”

—Winona Ryder, *Huffington Post*

“Well, it’s just one terrible memory that replays every time I have a moment of insecurity. [My classmates] would stand around me in a circle and they would jump on my back one by one and they would chant, ‘Ride the oaf. Ride the oaf.’”

—Jason Segel, *Hollywood.com*

“I had girls egging my home, writing curse words on the sidewalk in paint—just saying really nasty things about me. I quit cheerleading because I didn’t know what I was cheering for anymore! I grew up in that fishbowl of always being judged and watched. I really do believe that God was preparing me for the life I am living now.”

—Jessica Simpson, *Women’s Health Conference 2010*

"I've had experiences in middle school and high school with a bully. And I feel like when I was going through it, I was thinking, 'Well, maybe if I could help someone later on, then this will make it all worth it.' And individually, I think everyone should remember that. Your struggles will help others and you can get through it. You are not alone in this. There are so many people going through the same thing or have been through it, and it's really important to reach out and just know that you are stronger than any voice that brings you down."

—Brittany Snow, *MTV*

"I was a nerd in those days. Outsider. Like the kid that played the clarinet in the band and orchestra, which I did."

—Steven Spielberg, *60 Minutes*

"Junior high was actually sort of hard because I got dumped by this group of popular girls. They didn't think I was cool or pretty enough, so they stopped talking to me. The kids thought it was weird that I liked country [music]. They'd make fun of me. [Later on, the same girls] showed up [to my concert], wearing my T-shirts and asking me to sign their CDs. It was bittersweet, because it made me realize that they didn't remember being mean to me and that I needed to forget about it, too. Really, if I hadn't come home from school miserable every day, maybe I wouldn't have been so motivated to write songs. I should probably thank them!"

—Taylor Swift, *Teen Vogue*

"I wore really nerdy glasses because I was blind as could be, and the boys didn't like me. I actually got a lot of the mean girl stuff from the ages of 7 to 12. I was pretty much a mess in primary school."

—Charlize Theron, *People Magazine*

"I grew up in Tennessee, and if you didn't play football, you were a sissy. I got slurs all the time because I was into music and art. . . . I was an outcast in a lot of ways . . . but everything you get picked on for or you feel makes you weird is essentially what is going to make you sexy as an adult."

—Justin Timberlake, *Ellen*

Part I: Confidence

"Man often becomes what he believes himself
to be. If I keep on saying to myself that I
cannot do a certain thing, it is possible that I
may end up really becoming incapable of
doing it. On the contrary, if I have the belief
that I can do it, I shall surely acquire the
capacity to do it even if I may not have it at
the beginning."

—Mahatma Gandhi, Civil Rights Activist

Breaking the Cycle of Bullying

By Dorrell D. Palacio

"Nobody can hurt me without my
permission."
—Mahatma Gandhi, Peacekeeper

Bullying occurs in all shapes and sizes in every school around the country. Unfortunately, many children are familiar with bullying. For me, bullying started in early elementary school because I had trouble pronouncing certain words, and a few kids decided that my difference gave them permission to tease and harass me. I would go home upset and hurt, feeling that this bad treatment was just a part of life.

My mom raised my siblings and me by herself, but she was stronger than most married couples I knew. She would always tell me, "Everybody is different. Everyone was raised differently, and that is a good thing." Since my mom raised me to be so open-minded toward other people, it was confusing to me why others would pick on someone based on their differences. I wanted the situation to change immediately, so I set my mind to finding a solution. When my brother introduced me to mixed martial arts, I knew I had found my answer.

I walked into this environment of gladiators and warriors unconfident, scrawny, and unsure of my goals in life. As soon as I became persistent in my commitment to train and improve physically, I realized it wasn't just a physical goal I was reaching. Mixed martial arts was creating a level of confidence in myself that I never knew could exist. I became self-assured and confident, and I held my head high without any doubt in my eyes. Soon after, my skills in jiu-jitsu, judo, and boxing improved to the degree that I no longer feared going to school. When those same kids confronted me, I stood up for myself and didn't let them push me around anymore. I could see in their eyes that they knew they weren't messing with the same defenseless child. They were encountering a warrior who would not allow the cruelty of bullying to continue.

Soon after that the bullying rapidly faded, more quickly than I thought possible. My bullies had fed off of my fear and helplessness. When I got rid of those negative emotions, they had nothing else to feed off of when they saw me. Going into my middle and high school years, I was a totally different person. Mixed martial arts gave me a second chance at finding and standing up for myself. I continued to stand up, not only for myself, but also for anyone else whom bullying affected in the public school system.

I continued training and even started competing in various tournaments, which built my physical and mental strength. I learned that bullying doesn't have to be a part of anyone's life. I began setting high goals for myself because I knew that if I could overcome bullying early in my life, I could do anything I set my mind on. I gained the clarity, discipline, and confidence that would eventually lead me to go to school to attain my career goal as a paramedic for SWAT. I want to help and protect others in their most vulnerable times of need. I encourage anyone who has been or is presently a victim of bullying to let others know so you, too, can move forward in your life. You are not alone. Other people all around you are more than willing to help you.

About the Author

Dorrell D. Palacio is a college student with a passion for the martial arts. He practices kickboxing, judo, jiu-jitsu, and Muay Thai.

A Taste of Bullying

By S. Crossley

"If you want to live a happy life, tie it to a
goal, not to people or things."
—Albert Einstein, Physicist

I was seven years old when I had my first taste of bullying. . . . At my mother's insistence, I changed to a new school. She had heard some rumors about issues at my old school, and a different school in our area had a better reputation. While I wasn't happy about switching schools, I made a few friends, and academically there was no real change in what we were learning. I don't remember how the dream started, but I do know that by this point I had dreamed of being an athlete for years. A World Champion or an Olympian. At my old school, I had been part of a collection of teams and clubs, had felt confident to go out at lunchtime and play games with other people. No one had ever questioned my dream.

Until that day. For some unknown reason—probably something totally arbitrary—a boy at my new school took a particularly intense dislike to me. I'd never really experienced being disliked before, so at first I didn't understand what was going on. He took every opportunity to call me names and make fun of me, and slowly I felt him wearing away my spirit, taking away my will to try. He was unrelenting and pernicious, and his favorite topic was my weight.

Obviously I had always enjoyed sports, but suddenly every time I tried to participate in P.E. class, he was laughing at me. Soon other people joined in, too. They told me "fat people don't do sports" and "people who jiggle shouldn't run." Now, I had always been an overweight child, but it had never hindered me in any way, and therefore it had never bothered me. I still did everything I wanted to do, played any sport that took my fancy, and was decent or even good at most of them. I tried not to let the words get to me, but over time people started to exclude me from their games. I no longer got to join in soccer at lunchtime. I started being picked later and later for teams until I became resigned to the fact that I was going to be picked last.

To their credit, my teachers always tried to quash the poor behavior. They stopped letting us choose teams in P.E. class and started dividing us themselves. But of course, as they tend to do, my bullies found new ways of getting around the new arrangement. They started groaning and complaining whenever they got "stuck" with me. Soon they were refusing to pass me the ball or to even let me have a turn at the games. Most of my classmates were pleasantly surprised to find out I was actually an asset to the team when I was given a chance, but all too often I wasn't given an opportunity to show them.

Coming from a small school, I was saddled with these classmates for the next three years. Luckily, I made friends with some good people, and I didn't have a completely awful time at school, but there is something about those unpleasant people that sticks in the back of my mind to this day. It's always the negative words that stick with us, in the end, and those boys will never really be gone from my thoughts. They were the boys who convinced me that my dream was stupid and unachievable. The ones who made me automatically tell people I wasn't good at sports or didn't enjoy them. They were the ones who got me in trouble when I injured my ankle at my secondary school because they told everyone I was faking it so I didn't have to run.

It took a long time to recover my self-esteem from those experiences. For many years, I changed my answer when people asked what I wanted to do when I grew up. Instead of just telling them I wanted to be a World Champion, I felt as though I had to keep that dream a shameful secret and was compelled to answer that I wanted to do something more sedentary—that I wanted to work with computers or sit in an office. No matter how much I wanted to tell them, "I want to swim and dance and kick a ball. I want to fill my house with gold medals," I always had to stop and think first—to lie and make something up or answer, "I don't know."

It has been over ten years since that period of my life, and at least five since I last saw any of those people. Now I spend most of my time in the sports industry. I work daily teaching kids swimming and gymnastics—kids who don't care that I am still a "big" girl. In fact, I've had a few overweight children come through our classes who are tentative at first, but surprised and pleased that I can hold their weight on a bar or lift them out of the pool. It still makes me sad to see these kids who are the same age or younger than I was when my bullying started, but it also makes me proud and satisfied to know that I might have helped change their perspective. After all, if they can watch me do it, why can't they do it themselves?

I'm also actively involved in martial arts, instructing four classes a week and taking two of my own. That's over ten hours a week that I get to do something I love, something I am good at, and where I can help other people grow as athletes and as people. This year I will be sitting for my black belt test, and next year I will trial for the national team with a shot at competing in the World Championships.

Finally, after investing a lot of dedication and hard work, I have the chance to make my dream come true—even though I had started to think I never could. Bullying is never an easy experience to go through, but if you have the dedication and determination to get through it, there's no reason you can't achieve everything you want to achieve. Use their words to make you strong, learn to be unashamedly stubborn, and don't let anyone get you down.

About the Author

S. Crossley is a freelance writer and copy editor and a sports teacher. She has a talent for math and physics, and frequently volunteers her time with local competitive robotics groups. She is an avid martial artist, swimmer, and dancer.

She taught herself to read as a toddler and never stopped doing so, and began writing stories while her peers were learning the alphabet. She has published articles and short stories on various online media sites as well as in a national martial arts magazine.

S. Crossley was born in New Zealand and is currently still living in the town where she grew up.

Getting Free

By Kira Freed

"If you want things to change, do something
different."
—Anonymous

Being bullied has shaped my life in immeasurable ways. I was bullied
in my family as well as later at school. When I was eight, after a move
from the country to the city, bullying became a constant presence in
my life. I had hoped that my new school could offer a respite from
the hell of my home life, but it only added to it.

My parents weren't by nature cruel or completely unaware—in
fact, they were social activists who were involved in many progressive
causes. I was fortunate to be exposed to their forward-thinking values
at a time when many people were advocating ignorance and
prejudice. But the discrepancy between how they acted out in the
world and at home was crazy-making. I was expected to be obedient
within my family but a feisty activist everywhere else. I was allowed to
get angry about racial discrimination and the Vietnam War but was
expected to keep silent about my father's abuse.

Enduring years of my father's rage conditioned me to a life of
hypervigilance, reading his every facial expression, gesture, and tone
of voice in hopes of defusing his moods before they escalated into
violence. Although I rarely perceived any connection between my
actions and his explosions, I quickly learned that silence and supreme

obedience were smart strategies. By the time I reached my teens, fear had become so sufficient a control mechanism that he needed only to shoot me a steely glare and I was as well behaved as a beaten dog.

In my most vivid memory of his violence, he pulled down my pants and whipped me with his belt. I have no idea what I might have done to provoke his rage, and no sense of what any child could do to deserve that treatment. I only remember being a terror-stricken rag doll, helpless in the presence of his tall, muscled frame. Around the same time, my brother and I were in the kitchen one evening, bickering as we washed the dinner dishes. Our father burst into the room, shoved Mark into a corner, and struck him hard several times. I crouched in the opposite corner, frozen in fear, praying to become invisible so I could evade my father's tornadic fury, yet compelled to witness the violence in order to burn into my memory the consequences of crossing him.

My mother objected to my father's treatment of my brother, younger sister, and me, but she did nothing to stop it. She would tsk-tsk, shake her head in disapproval, and claim to be the peace-loving parent, even though she abused one of my older sisters. My mother was rarely violent toward me—nothing more than a few whacks with a hairbrush once in a while—but she was relentless in claiming to know what was best for me and forcing her agendas on me. I was, and still am, a devout tomboy and a fiercely independent thinker. Although she claimed to be a champion of women's rights and told me I could grow up to be any kind of woman I wanted to be, she prodded me nonstop to be more feminine and compliant. She also slammed my opinions and actions if they didn't agree with hers. She once told me I was "on a path to self-destruction" because I enjoyed reading children's books when I was in college and wasn't shaping up to be scholarly like her. Writing children's books is now my main career.

My siblings were no picnic, either. My oldest sister, who bossed me around like a little dictator, felt like a malevolent parasite I could never escape. My next-oldest sister once smashed the door of a metal mailbox on my fingers because I reached for the mail before she did. (I still have a scar.) My brother rigged a hammer on the crossbar of our swing set and convinced me to sit in the swing; it's a miracle my skull wasn't fractured when the hammer fell on my head. My younger sister pounded me brutally with her fists whenever she was angry with me. And, in truth, I acted in very controlling ways toward my younger sister. I feel remorse for how I behaved, and I also recognize that none of us had a prayer of growing up emotionally healthy; we were all acting out our distress from being raised in an abusive home. Yet my parents regularly told us that we were lucky to grow up in such a wonderful family.

When I was young, trusting my own perceptions and preserving my sense of self in the face of the abuse and contradictory messages was a monumental task. A large part of my ability to stay connected to myself was thanks to the natural world and a particular nonhuman friend.

When I was fourteen, my parents bought some land in a secluded valley. Before long, my father was given two horses that he boarded with a neighbor. Boomer was a huge, exquisitely gentle chestnut on whose back I learned to ride—to meld with his powerful energy and guide him using my newly discovered body intuition.

The safety of my connection with Boomer eased my hypervigilance and provided me with a kinesthetic experience of trust that counteracted the all-too-familiar climate of abuse and fear. Whereas my father could turn on me without warning, Boomer was constant, loyal, and kind. He honored my need for gentleness without compromising his strength, and not only served as my surrogate father during those years but also provided me with a template for intimacy that continues to serve me well. I learned from Boomer that strength and gentleness, far from being polar opposites, are a wonderful blend.

Boomer was my lifeline during my teen years, and therapy kept me sane during my twenties and beyond. Being in therapy has been by far the best decision of my life. It has given me a space to explore my feelings and truths, a window outside the extreme dysfunction of my family, and an enduring experience of being treated with kindness and respect. Recovering from bullying and abuse is a lifelong process, for me at least, and I continue to work with a therapist as needed.

The other things that have made a huge difference in my life have been learning about healthy boundaries (I highly recommend Susan Campbell's books *Getting Real* and *Saying What's Real*) and moving far away from my family. Over time, as the strife between us continued, I severed my relationships with them. Separating from my family isn't a choice I made lightly, and it's not for everyone, but staying connected took too great a toll on me. Out of a sense of responsibility for my own well-being, I decided not to put myself through that kind of treatment any longer. I call it a radical act of self-care.

However, there's been one shining exception with regard to family relationships. Before my father died in 1991 and immediately after, I went through a remarkable healing process that helped me find my voice and also healed my hard feelings toward him. In addition, it healed my inner template for men, which finally allowed me to have a healthy intimate relationship. I'm left with deep, openhearted love for my father, which I never would have predicted or even dreamed of, based on my painful early history with him.

Sometimes I can't quite believe how good my life is now. I wake up next to my sweet, gentle husband, look around at my peaceful home, and tell myself, "This is my life. I'm safe now." I marvel at the fact that I do work I love—mainly writing nonfiction books for educational publishers, many about overcoming injustice—and that my life is drama-free, abuse-free, and profoundly satisfying. I survived. I escaped the prison of my childhood, and I walked away from continuing mistreatment by family members and others. That's definitely something to celebrate.

Over time, I've learned to take the long view of the experiences that have shaped my life. Without either minimizing my pain or excusing the perpetrators, I've come to acknowledge the gifts that have accompanied the mistreatment. I've developed a strong sense of boundaries and an absolute clarity about my right to follow my own path. I've learned to trust my inner wisdom above all else. I've discovered my resilience and have had the privilege of supporting others to develop theirs.

It's true that we don't always have choice over how people treat us, but we're free to choose how we want to respond. I have a framed note in a special place in my office that says, "I get to choose." And I have another one that says, "I want to live a life as big as my capacities." No one gets to make me live a small life. They don't get a vote in who I am or the choices I make. I'm free.

You, too, can free yourself and live a life as big as your capacities. Find something to hold on to when things are tough—a friend (human or nonhuman), a bullying hotline, a support group, a hobby, a story of healing and empowerment, even a tree or a stuffed animal you can talk to (I did both for several years). Use everything on your path to grow and heal. Build your vision of a satisfying life, and get fierce about your right to make it a reality. Breathe fire as needed to make space for yourself in the world. Refuse to take no for an answer.

About the Author

Kira Freed is a freelance writer, mainly for educational publishers, as well as a licensed psychotherapist and certified life coach. She is the author of *Losing and Finding My Father: Seasons of Grief, Healing and Forgiveness*, a memoir about her remarkable journey of transformation following the death of her father.

No Safe Haven

By Ann Jamieson

"When I discover who I am, I'll be free."
—Ralph Ellison, Novelist

Bursting with flames, the four-foot-high garbage can came barreling down the stairway directly at me. Only by leaping over the banister to the lower set of stairs was I able to escape. It was no accident. They knew I would be passing down those stairs just at that moment to go to my next class. They were waiting for me.

That was the most terrifying incident of being bullied in my life. Of course, that was only one of the methods they used to strike fear in me. A gang of girls once surrounded me as I was trying to leave school. One of them grabbed my hair and held me, pulling it until I screamed, while the others moved in as though they were about to beat me up. Two school bus drivers intervened, but after that my mother picked me up from school every day, as it was not safe for me to walk home alone.

The school did nothing to reprimand the students. When my mother confronted them, they told her that I needed to work it out with the other students. Recess was safe only because two teachers kept watch over everyone.

Thwarted by their efforts to physically beat or burn me, the bullies changed tactics. They continued to torture me by stealing things off my desk and out of my pocketbook, grabbing it from me and taunting me by keeping it just out of my reach. Whenever the teacher was out of earshot, they would threaten to come to my house and beat me, or they would simply tell me they hated me and they were going to "get me" in some unspecified way. Because I was intelligent and liked to learn, I was labeled the "teacher's pet." Apparently that was a crime to them—a crime that needed punishing.

Making it worse for me was the fact that the bullying continued when I got home. No matter how hard I tried, no matter what I did, I was never good enough for my father. If I received a ninety-eight on my report card, he wanted to know where the other two points were. An "A" on an essay? "Why wasn't it an "A+?"

Comments about my looks were equally devastating. "You have a face like a horse," he would tell me. Or, "Your thighs look like sausages." At five feet six and with a weight that never went over 130 pounds in my life, I was scarcely fat, but that didn't stop him. Trying to protect me, my mother pleaded with him to stop. His response was to bully her, too.

Bullying destroys a person's self-confidence, makes mincemeat of his or her self-esteem. Believing that I couldn't do anything right, I started to live that truth. I flunked math; I dropped out of a science course.

Life became terrifying, and everything made me anxious. It got so bad that I would wake up in the morning shaking. I didn't want to get out of bed or go to school. I would scream and cry and fight to stay home. My mother took me to the doctor, but he couldn't find anything wrong. Bullying wasn't discussed back then.

Going away to college helped. No one attempted to bully me there, and I was at last away from my father's incessant criticism. In fact, my English professors praised my work and encouraged me to make a career out of writing. This encouragement, combined with living away from my father, made college one of the happiest times of my life.

Once I was home again, it all began anew. While trying to develop a career writing articles for magazines and newspapers, I went through one low-paying job after another. Fired for not promoting dessert at a Hardee's restaurant, for not serving coffee fast enough at a mall coffee shop, and for prepping too slowly at a Pizza Hut, all my old demons returned. I was worthless, I couldn't do anything right, I would never be successful. My father, I thought, was right.

Although I enjoyed writing and had several articles published, the $60 or so that I would earn could hardly sustain me, so I remained at home.

In a matter of years, I went through at least thirty jobs. Each failure reinforced my father's words. I was not good enough. He harassed me continually. "When are you going to get a good job? I put you through college—now you're wasting your life."

Floundering in bad jobs, bad relationships, and suicidal thoughts, I hit bottom. Not only was I down, but people seemed to keep kicking me while I was there.

Thankfully, I did find a way out, through a combination of techniques. Over time, I created a protocol to heal myself. (I had tried therapy, and I know it works for some people, but for me it wasn't a success. Perhaps it was merely a lack of finding the right therapist.)

Making a list of things that made me happy, I came up with writing, riding horses, my cats, nature, and reading. I had always loved horses. I had taken lessons, and I started riding at my instructor's barn. While I was there, I was happy. And I could ride—I had talent. Instead of criticism, I found encouragement. Selling my flute and my bicycle, I bought a horse.

My horse and my writing took me away from the pain of being "not good enough." When I rode and when I wrote, I *was* good enough. In another world where none of the hurt from the bullies could reach me, I excelled.

Reading positive books, listening to tapes of speakers such as Norman Vincent Peale and Robert Schuller (who affirmed the innate goodness of people), riding my horse, and writing all eased my anxiety and helped me discover my worth. Spending time in nature and marveling at its beauty made me feel part of something bigger—something wonderful.

I meditate now, although I can't quite sit still and "not think of anything." Instead, I listen to guided meditations. Nature and meditation help calm my battered psyche. I found friends and a spiritual center where people love me unconditionally. I can make mistakes, and it's no big deal. They accept me because, after all, everyone makes mistakes.

I think the paths we take to bring ourselves back to wholeness, to believe that we are worthy, and to regain the things that bullying robbed from us will probably all be different. But I'm living proof that it is possible. Combining my loves of writing and horses, I am now a much in-demand horse-show judge and a writer of books and articles about horses and travel (another love I've discovered).

I am truly reborn, and I believe all bullying victims can reclaim the lives they were meant to lead.

About the Author

Ann Jamieson is a United States Equestrian Federation judge licensed in hunters, jumpers, and hunt seat equitation. She has had the privilege of judging the Vermont Finals twice and the Massachusetts Finals once.

Ann has written numerous articles for magazines and newspapers, including a column for the award-winning regional paper *The Litchfield County Times*. She currently writes for *Today's Equestrian* magazine, a regional publication focused on the New York/New Jersey/Connecticut area. She loved the *All Creatures Great and Small* books, which proved to be the inspiration behind her popular series *For the Love of the Horse*.

She lives in Connecticut with her two cats and an assortment of tropical fish.

Growing from the Inside

By Anonymous

"It's never too late to be who you might have been."

—George Eliot, Author

As a professional litigator, it's difficult to imagine a time when I wasn't assertive, yet that's exactly how I used to be as a child. If I got teased, I took it—and I got teased a lot. Although you couldn't see it, I had scars, the kind that were beneath the surface and deep-rooted. They made me who I am today—a loving and confident person who has done more than I could have ever anticipated.

How It Began

The teasing began in sixth grade and continued throughout most of high school. I suppose it had to do with my religion being different from that of the majority of the people around me. Growing up in Staten Island, there were very few other Jewish people.

When I was in sixth grade, I wasn't in the popular clique. Luckily, I found friends—outsiders like me who were also in need of friends. Back then, I got picked on because I was thin and considered unattractive. I once overheard a boy I liked say I'd look better with a shorter nose since my nose "cast a huge shadow." Although he didn't say it to my face, the words stung.

In junior high school, I was still a skinny kid but tried to make myself look pretty so I'd feel better about myself. Every morning before school, I set my hair with hot curlers, which took thirty minutes. I then styled my mid-length hair in the then-current style so that it curled in at the bottom. I wore clothes that were considered cool back then, like go-go boots and miniskirts. Everything was color coordinated and accessorized. I had an eye for fashion, but none of it helped.

Unfortunately, my efforts were in vain. In front of the entire ninth-grade cafeteria, one boy took it upon himself to call me flat chested on a regular basis. Normal folks might be repelled by such rudeness. But like metal pulled to a magnet, I kept sitting near him every day. The irony was that our fathers were both doctors and socialized with each other. Finally, one day I had had enough of his insults and moved to another side of the cafeteria, but I endured his verbal abuse for two months before moving. Why I put up with his offensive behavior every day is beyond me except that I loved his British accent and had a crush on him. I detested him after I moved my seat.

In my junior year of high school, my family moved from Staten Island to a northern suburb of New York. I didn't know anyone at the school, and I still wasn't popular, but thankfully I wasn't being teased. There was more diversity there, so I finally felt as though I fit in, at least in some small way. I was grateful to blend into the crowd.

On a family trip to Hawaii that year, we were walking in Waikiki when a local boy shouted out, "Hey, there's the girl with the skinny legs." I was humiliated but knew the reference. Joe Tex had done a song called "Skinny Legs and All" that referred to "the girl with the skinny legs"—a line in Paul Revere and the Raiders' version of "Boogaloo Down Broadway." People today would pray to have skinny legs, but back then it was something nobody wanted to hear because it was considered a put-down.

Even though I still felt unattractive, I had a few boyfriends and went to the ninth-grade prom and the senior prom. In my junior year, there was a boy in my class who had a big crush on me, but he was shy and we never dated. Still, it was nice to know someone could have a crush on me for a change.

Despite all of this, I was unhappy in my own skin. I had become very self-conscious from all the teasing. I finally had my nose fixed in my senior year before the prom. It was something I had wanted to do. It made a huge difference in my confidence—temporarily.

When I started college, I gained seven pounds, which also made a world of difference. I wasn't skinny anymore. I was just the right weight and shape. People said they wished they were thin like me. It felt good to be complimented, but again, those feelings were only temporary.

With my newfound looks, I thought the bullying was over, but it wasn't. There was still something missing inside. During the summer, I had an experience that would change my perception of the world. I worked at a camp for two summers. During the second year, the owner retired and his nasty son took over. He was surly and lacked his father's warmth. The son was the camp bully, picking on everyone, including the counselors. Working for him made me miserable, so I quit a week early. I expected my mother to pick me up the next day, but I was mistaken.

The night I quit, I was on the phone with my boyfriend. I was nineteen at the time. We had an argument, but I had to end the call because I had to get to girls' camp before curfew. I was five minutes late but figured it didn't matter because I had already quit. Wrong— the son made an example of counselors who quit, so I was told I would be awakened the next morning at 6:00 A.M. and put on a bus to New York City. I didn't even have money for the bus. I had to wake up my uncle, the camp doctor, to borrow money. He and my aunt yelled at me for embarrassing them, which added to my humiliation and anger. I borrowed the money and got on the bus after hugging my campers goodbye. That was the beginning of my transformation.

Transformation

For a long time, I thought about that last day of camp and how I didn't know my legal rights. If I had, I would have known that the camp didn't have the right to put me on a bus.

I started researching it a year later and discovered that I could have stayed at the edge of the property and that they couldn't force me to get on the bus. I was furious with them—and with myself for allowing them to do that to me. That was it, I said. No more. No more trampling on my rights, no more taking garbage from anyone who thinks it's okay to hurt me. In fact, now I won't even take it from family members. I have actually walked away from family members, including cousins and aunts, because I refuse to be stepped on.

In college, I started thinking about going to law school. My college boyfriend was going to law school, and he and I were competitive with each other. Additionally, my mother said on one occasion that I'd make a good lawyer. That stayed with me.

I applied to law school and was accepted. I started out in Ohio and then transferred to a law school in New York. Transferring law schools was unheard of then, but I wanted to take the New York bar and was learning Ohio law. As a determined individual, I passed the New York bar on my first attempt and worked for a few law firms before starting my own firm. Since 2001, I have been a sole practitioner, specializing in family law and appeals.

Looking back, sometimes it almost seems a shame that I moved away from Staten Island. I have come a long way. Since finding my confidence, I have been able to accomplish a lot without worrying too much about what other people think. The energy inside of me was looking for a way out. Today, I am a freelance writer, published author, and published poet. I have a poetry website where I create custom poems for all occasions. I'm also a professional musician and am in a gigging band playing piano, keyboards, organ, and synthesizer. My husband plays saxophone in the band. Sometimes my daughter, a sax player, joins us. I've been in bands for the last twelve years and don't intend to stop anytime soon. In my spare time, I'm at my crafts workbench making silk flower arrangements or something with sea glass. I also have a photography website that's under construction, but I expect that my husband, an IT guy and photographer, will work on it with me soon

I have two terrific children and a great stepson. My husband? He's the boy who had the crush on me in my junior year of high school. We found each other after thirty years and have been happily married for the last twelve.

Metamorphosis

My transformation came about because I had an epiphany that I didn't deserve to be hurt. I discovered I had rights and wanted to learn more about them, so I went to law school. I promised myself I would never allow anyone to step on me again. I learned that just because you're different, you don't deserve to be treated differently.

Along the way, I developed a guarded attitude that has served me well. I'm cynical and am not quick to make a friend until I know I can trust that person. I could have let these experiences ruin my life, but they didn't. I learned from them and grew as a person. Everyone is hurt to some extent—some more than others. If we allow the pain to consume us, we will always be stuck in that awful place.

I also found someone to talk to. It happened to be my biology teacher who was willing to listen. He helped me gain the confidence I lacked. The cosmetic changes didn't create the assertive person I am today—talking things out and figuring out how to protect myself created the new, assertive me. It took some time to get there, but I've never looked back.

About the Author

The author is a professional writer and lawyer specializing in family appeals. She lives with her husband and daughter in New York City and has practiced law for over thirty-five years.

To Be Like the Cool Kids

By Candace McAfee

"Being cool is being your own self, not doing something that someone else is telling you to do."

—Vanessa Hudgens, Actress

As I was growing up, the adults in my family assured me that bullying was a part of life. "Not everyone is going to like you, Candace," my mom used to say. "Sometimes people just can't find a way to get along." While I knew that was probably true, I just couldn't understand why some kids were downright mean, while others were friendly and great to play with. I liked my group of friends, but I wasn't popular. That was okay with me since the popular girls always seemed to be getting in trouble.

The "leader of the pack" was a beautiful girl named Ashley who was always dressed in the best clothes thanks to her older sisters. She was the youngest of five girls, and her older sisters obviously doted on her. Ashley's best friend was a girl named Lisa, who had been my bully since the first grade. Like Ashley, Lisa also had an older sister, but unlike Ashley, Lisa's sister was mean. She had a big group of friends, three grades above us, who liked to threaten and intimidate anyone they didn't like. Unfortunately for me, I was the one Lisa didn't like, and I'd already had a run-in with her sister and her friends in third grade. They surrounded me on the playground and corralled me onto the baseball field, calling me names and kicking dirt all over me. That year, despite my incident with the sixth graders, things really turned around for me. I auditioned for the school play and was the youngest cast member with a lead role! When my classmates found out I was good at singing and acting, suddenly they all seemed to want to be my friends.

The following year, I landed the role of Dorothy in *The Wizard of Oz*. My dream role! I was so happy. Ashley was cast as Glenda, the Good Witch, so we spent a lot of time together at rehearsals. Over the next few months, we actually became friends, realizing we would be in the same Girl Scout troop in fifth grade. Summer arrived quickly and school ended.

Over the break, my body began to change. I took books out of the library about puberty to learn what in the world was happening to me. The books explained that most girls didn't begin this stage until they were in their early teens; however, it was possible for younger girls to begin as early as ten. "I'm ten!" I cried. I just knew that when school was back in session, everyone would notice how different I looked, and it would be a disaster.

My mom readied me with a shopping spree at J. C. Penney. I stocked up on the cutest outfits, platform shoes, and trendy hats. My first day of school felt as though I was in a teen movie—it seemed that every popular kid knew my name! For the first time in my life, no one teased me or had anything terrible to say. At lunch, it was all compliments and saved seats, all except for Lisa. Lisa had been dismissed from her eternal seat next to Ashley, at Ashley's request! I thought my friend was being rude and mean, but I wasn't sure what to say. Lisa went to sit alone, and I took her seat. It wasn't long before I realized that the girls who were my new "best friends" were still just as mean as they had been before, only now my bully was "out" and I was "in." I felt terrible about it, and I knew I had to move on, even though Lisa was just the *worst*.

I was popular for one year in my entire life, and it was one of the worst years I ever had in primary school. I knew those girls and saw the issues and sadness they dealt with that typically came from one another—girls who were supposed to be their friends. I saw girls dig deeper and deeper into rebellion, bullying their enemies, friends, and families. As a result, I learned to not listen so closely to what they had to say about me. I began to notice that being confident in myself and comfortable with my differences, while still being nice to others, really went a long way. I never really felt bullied again, and I found that speaking out against bullying in the moment can really change things for the better.

Even adults can sometimes experience bullying. Some people dislike the person they are, and the only way they can feel better about themselves is to hurt others. That is their problem, not yours. You are here to be you, to live a great life, and to do wonderful things. You are here to make a difference. Maybe the difference you'll make will help someone else!

About the Author

Candace McAfee is thirty, flirty, and thriving. A stepmother to two lovely children, partner to a dreamy toy designer, and human to a precocious black cat, Candace enjoys book snobbery, cosplaying, silly walks, and cup collecting. She also prefers her snozzberries to taste like snozzberries.

Life Can Be Hard for an Introvert

By David A. Machine

"True self-esteem comes from confidence,
not the other way around." —Susan Cain,
Lecturer

Introduction

As a child, I was very sensitive, curious, and introverted. While other kids were playing baseball, I liked to read. I was very interested in science and had a lot of ideas about the world that I loved to talk about, but my peers could not understand, so I was labeled *weird*. I didn't care, for the most part, but I also wanted to fit in, so I stopped talking about ideas and dumbed myself down to fit in a little better. It wasn't cool to be smart.

I didn't watch *Charlie's Angels*. It was every boy's favorite TV show in the 1970s—three female private investigators whose boss, Charlie, got them into adventures every week. What was the point? A TV show about three women I would never meet? And who were fifteen or twenty years older than me anyway? They would be interested in a little boy? What were they, female pedophiles? So then I was told I was homosexual. Not in those words. I was called a *fag*, a *queer*, and *gay*.

Middle school was worse. I got thick glasses and was promptly dubbed *four-eyes* and *geek*. I was targeted by seven kids in particular. There were two groups of three that I was an endless source of amusement for. In one group, you had the leader—let's call him Stan*—a mean, angry kid well acquainted with violence, poverty, and hardship. You had Pete, who had little will of his own; he was a follower who just did as the others told him to. The last one of the bunch was Mark, a quiet kid who kept to himself in seventh grade. Something happened to him over the summer, and day after day in eighth grade, he wore the same clothes, which became tattered. Maybe his parents divorced and he was left with a mother who couldn't support him. At any rate, something went wrong in his life.

The other group was led by Ralph, his follower, Jim, and a sadist named Terry. Didn't they ever just get tired of it? The seventh bully was the very epitome of intimidation. He was adult size by age fifteen—he may have been held back a year. He was about five feet ten and 180 pounds, with thick, muscled arms and a big chest. Violence was a very serious matter for him. When he walked down the hall, people moved out of his way. Everyone in the school feared him, including most of the teachers. He scared me. I thought he might kill me. He carried a knife and had a reputation as a fighter who "could take it, not just dish it out." I was skinny and shy, and wore glasses, so girls didn't pay much attention to me, and I wasn't going to bother approaching any of them. I was realistic. Once again, my peers interpreted this as *gay*.

When I was a freshman in high school, I shot up to six foot two, but the rest of me had not caught up yet. I weighed 120 pounds. The net result was that I looked like a stick figure. I wore even thicker glasses. I was weak, slow, and poorly coordinated. It was open season on me. I would be slapped, punched, grabbed, tripped, pushed, threatened, mocked, insulted, and humiliated every day. Telling my parents would do no good. My father was very disturbed and a drug addict who had grown increasingly irrational and angry over the years. My mother was preoccupied with tending to him, so I was neglected and forgotten. Tell the principal or teachers? They would call the bullies in for a talk, and then the bullies would pay me back by mistreating and abusing me worse. Fight back? They would have put me in the hospital. And I probably would have gotten suspended for fighting upon discharge from the emergency room. There was nowhere safe. Not at home, not at school.

Do you know how hard it is to do homework with a crazy man on drugs in the next room, yelling threats and insults at you and your mother? It is rather distracting. I gave up on homework and failed most of my classes. *Loser*, *Dummy*, and *Retard* were added to my monikers.

In school, I would sit in class with my head down, my chin resting on my hand, full of shame and fear, not saying a word, trying not to be noticed, which made me even more noticeable. I had few friends. I felt ashamed and disgusted with myself and extremely fearful of abuse from my peers. Walking home, I would get a knot in my stomach that would get worse as I got closer to my house. I never knew what to expect when I got home. Sunday night I would get a sick feeling in my stomach, knowing I would have to go to school the next day and face more abuse and mistreatment. That was my life.

Growth and Development

High school eventually ended. I swallowed my shame at being so weak that I was afraid to go to a gym and found that I wanted to become stronger. I started going to the YMCA and lifting weights. Nobody there picked on me. All the huge guys either kept to themselves and left me alone or took an interest in the scrawny, emaciated kid who wanted to improve himself and taught me how to lift more safely and effectively. What a difference it made. In three months, I put on about twenty-five pounds of muscle. I got a job at a lumberyard and started college. I barely graduated high school, so my choices for college were very limited. I took a class at an open-enrollment community college. I started soaking up the experience. I was in an environment where being smart was finally valued and where reading and studying were expected. I got to listen to and talk about ideas. *Geek* and *nerd* were no longer fitting labels—it was cool to be smart. At the lumberyard, I learned I could actually do things; I was not a *loser*, *dummy*, or *retard*. Girls started paying attention to me, and I reciprocated. I became more confident, and my anxiety levels and shame diminished. When I finally got my own apartment, I drove over a bridge, left my terrible home behind, and headed for my new home. A thought came into my head in the middle of the bridge: "I am going to experience so much personal growth and development now that I am away from those people [my family]." I had no idea how much I would be able to accomplish once I was away from those destructive influences.

Today

Since then, I finished college, went to graduate school, and continued body building, and later, running and cross-training. I enjoyed the company of some beautiful ladies and good friends as well as freedom, autonomy, and independence as a result of being away from abusive people. I developed a degree of competence and confidence. I learned to assert myself—but I went to extremes at times, and my boundaries were sometimes terrible. For a while, it was a daily battle to not go to either extreme of passivity or aggression. I search for the middle ground of assertiveness, so I neither run people over and feel guilty and ashamed or let myself get run over and then hate myself and feel ashamed. I have realized that fear is okay—a certain amount of it can keep you safe, and Hollywood-inspired macho bullshit gets people hurt, crippled, dead, sued, or in jail. I feel less ashamed as I realize this. I also realize the courage it took to keep going to a place where I got my ass kicked day after day—middle school and high school—and to face reality without using drugs and alcohol to go numb. I have embraced my introversion and realized it is okay to prefer your own company and enjoy solitude and quiet. I value and take care of my body, and I read voraciously.

Since then, I have taught college courses in psychology, substance abuse, violence, criminology, and victimology, and I've evaluated and counseled about three thousand men, women, and juveniles who have had problems with some combination of addiction, violence, anger, criminal behavior, sex offenses, dealing or possessing drugs, burglary, other property crimes, vandalism, domestic assault, child abuse, delinquency, and victimization, including molestation and sexual assault. I have seen some of the worst aspects of human nature. I am no longer impressed with or intimidated by violent individuals. Swaggering loudmouths who think they are tough bore me or make me laugh. My career path has been largely influenced, if not directed, by the abuse I went through as a child and teen. Today I work to prevent violent individuals from victimizing others, and I help victims of violence cope and function better.

What You Can Do

- Seek professional assistance if your past is interfering with your present. Bullying can leave deep psychological scars that can interfere with your adult relationships and lead to substance abuse, PTSD, or suicidal behaviors. Don't try to cope with these problems on your own.

- Don't buy into the shame or accept the labels others have pasted on you. Realize that there is much more wrong with the bullies than with you. It is not normal to mercilessly torment and abuse someone else. Bullies have to hurt others in order to feel good about themselves. They are badly damaged individuals. The preoccupation many of the bullies have with sexual orientation has to do with their doubts and uncertainties about their own sexuality. They ridicule people with ideas they cannot understand, or those who value or cultivate intelligence, because they don't want anyone outdoing them. They abuse those who are weaker because they feel weak and out of control and have to externalize their lack of control by hurting others.

- A degree of conformity is required to live and work in a society, and appearance does matter. This is one of the many facets of human behavior that is so complicated. Preserve your integrity and be who you are, but don't draw unnecessary attention to yourself with outrageous appearance or behavior. Develop a neat and squared-away appearance.

- Weakness is a choice. You can do something about it. Develop your body. Strength training can help you in many ways. Your clothes will fit better, posture will improve, you will be able to tolerate stress better, anxiety will go down, your self-esteem and confidence will improve, and others may hesitate to target you for abuse.

- Find the middle ground between being submissive and aggressive. This middle ground is assertiveness. Submissiveness will encourage others to be aggressive toward you. Don't become aggressive toward others. It is easy to go to extremes and develop a "never again" attitude, as in "Never again will I be victimized." You may see threats where they don't exist and treat too many others as your enemy.

- If you are getting bullied now, focus on the future. Middle school and high school tend to be the worst times for bullying. It will pass. Start setting goals. Who and where do you hope to be one day?

- Find a mentor or support person. Having just one good friend or trusted adult to hear you, support you, and value you can make a very big difference in how you feel about yourself. I have one friend I have known since seventh grade whom I still talk to or email almost every day. He has helped me more than I can describe.

- Cultivate your knowledge and intelligence. Don't ever be ashamed of it. Learn as much as you can and develop skills. Prove to yourself that you are not dumb or helpless.

Conclusion

Being subjected to bullying can leave deep psychological scars, but the impact of bullying can be overcome. It will take hard work and determination on your part, but it can be done.

About the Author

David Machine is a college instructor, psychotherapist, and avid amateur athlete. He loves to run, lift weights, read, cook, take photos, learn, share ideas with others, and sometimes just sit and enjoy the silence and solitude.

Part II: Education

"I did then what I knew how to do. Now that

I know better,

I do better."

—Maya Angelou, Poet

The Turning Point

By Melina Adhikari

"Even if you keep the dog's tail underwater
for a decade,
it will still be curved. It will never straighten."

—Nepali proverb

Sarah, the only daughter of loving parents, was a girl of amazing enthusiasm and gigantic ambition. But being a member of the poorest of households meant that others would not necessarily treat her aspirations so kindly.

At twelve, Sarah attended the SOS Hermann Gmeiner School in Bharatpur, Nepal. The school had been founded in 1984 by the SOS Children's Villages organization, based in Austria. It was one of the oldest in Faridabad. The school's campus was designed by a German architect.

The school was home to a variety of children from all walks of life. They were united by one common feature—they were all destitute. Along with Sarah, the students included Rickie, Bella, and Jackie Smith. All three were eager to impress the headmistress, Mrs. Watson, who ran the school yard as a surrogate mother.

"What are you doing here?" one of the children demanded.

Taken by surprise, Sarah began to apologize. "I am sorry, but . . . "

"Just stay away from us and the others. You are the most horrible, unlucky person in the world," Rickie shouted.

Softhearted Sarah burst into tears. Running toward the changing room, she hid her face in her hands. This was the first of many days that Sarah would spend hiding. It was upsetting, but Sarah managed to stay optimistic and cheerful in spite of what her would-be detractors wanted.

But then the situation worsened. . . .

One day, Sarah's best friend, Aarushi, whose parents were as poor as hers, joined in with the bullies.

"Sarah is a box of bad luck with no self-esteem!" Aarushi said.

In Sarah's young heart, depression set in. The whole world seemed to close in on her. Even her beloved best friend had turned on her.

Suddenly, at twelve, Sarah was contemplating suicide. . . . She took the shawl she was wearing into a noose and stood on a stool, tying and tightening it to the ceiling fan. Taking a deep breath, which she hoped would be her last, she kicked the stool she was standing on. . . .

But her older sister, Bimala, walked in.

"NO NO NO!!! PLEASE DON'T DO THIS!! PLEASE PLEASE," she cried when she saw Sarah.

Bimala immediately detached Sarah from the fan and took her to the hospital. The doctors were thankfully able to revive her. When she finally recovered her strength, her parents and sister pressured her to admit what had happened.

Sarah confessed that she was being bullied. Her sister told her to try to be positive toward her bullies and maybe they would stop. Her parents were worried, but there was nothing they could do. They were a poor family—too poor to bear the expenses of other schools, as Sarah was on a scholarship. SOS was the least expensive school in Bharatpur.

Sarah decided then that it was terrible to have tried to commit suicide. There were so many people around her who loved her. What she was doing was caving in to the bullies, people who did not deserve to win. She made up her mind to find strength inside herself to cope.

Months later, her parents' friend, Tom England—a traveler from abroad whom they took in—introduced Sarah to the wonderful world of books and literature. Finding a passion in reading, Sarah focused on her education and enlightening her mind. She used reading as an outlet and an escape. For four years, she ignored her bullies and their taunts. They told her she was dumb, unlucky, and unworthy. But at eighteen, she became the valedictorian of SOS Hermann Gmeiner School, class of 2000.

Her ambitious attitude paid off, and now her dreams have come true. Despite all those who wished her ill, Sarah is pursuing her dreams. She found that when she stopped listening to the naysayers, she was able to make her wishes come true. So can you.

About the Author

Melina Adhikari currently works as a senior English teacher in Nepal and holds a master's degree in English language. She was the once-frustrated Sarah but is pleased to say that she has beaten her childhood bullies.

On Bullying

By Patricia Brown

"Knowing what's right doesn't mean much
unless you do
what's right."
—Theodore Roosevelt, Former President

Walking alone on the playground, I was usually okay with my own thoughts and dreams until I'd hear, "Smear the queer! That's YOU!" It would bring me out of my little world and back into the nightmare of school and all those horrible children I wanted nothing to do with. I felt extremely isolated and lonely, as though no one cared, because no one did.

Coming from a dysfunctional home with two messed-up parents didn't help. My dad was an alcoholic who was rarely home, but when he was, I did what I could to stay out of his way. He was a bully in his own right, threatening me and telling me how fat I was. My mom was never around because she was too busy trying to make money to pay the bills since my dad couldn't hold down a job. Had she been there, she wouldn't have cared enough to ask about school anyway. I was the child who shouldn't have happened. I had no one to talk to, no one to help me with the hurt. I was all alone—something I would experience for many years.

As I got older, things just got worse. Occasionally a new kid would come to school, and I would reach out and have the temporary companionship I so longed for until they, too, would turn on me. Then I quit reaching out, knowing how it would end up. I longed for someone, anyone, in my life. Eventually I turned to books. Reading allowed me to see what a friendship would really be like and how people should treat each other. The characters in my books became my friends—true friends who wouldn't say mean things or tell me I was a freak.

As time passed, the imaginary friends helped, but they couldn't take away the pain. I was lonely, depressed, miserable, and getting older. Kids can be cruel, and it felt as though life would never get better. For me, it would be a long time before it would. I had to deal with threats from people who wanted to beat me up, kids making fun of me in front of entire classrooms, and the isolation, which was the worst part of all.

When high school came around, I wasn't excited like most kids, for obvious reasons. It would just be three more long years of hating my existence. Although I still found some solace in books at that point, I started feeling different and felt as though I couldn't take it anymore. I just didn't want to live. There was no point.

I thought long and hard about killing myself, and I guess in a way I became obsessed with death. I welcomed it, begged for it, but no matter the method I thought of, I just didn't have the guts when it came to doing it. As much as I wanted to die, I just couldn't do that to myself.

As a young adult not knowing where to turn or what to do, I

found myself becoming friends with people who finally accepted me. And in return for their friendship, I did drugs with them. Although I'm not proud of it, I understand why I did it and don't fault myself for needing some kind of escape that took me years to overcome. Knowing that really wasn't me or who I wanted to be, I finally got some help. I went to a psychiatrist who told me that imagining people in books were my friends wasn't all that crazy, and that many people turn to drugs to take pain away. He put me on some antidepressants, and after about six weeks I felt better than I had in a long time. I was finally able to get my life together.

I went to college and wound up teaching at an elementary school where I witnessed bullying on a daily basis. The difference was, I was no longer a quiet, shy, fragile little girl who was an easy target. I was in charge.

I would immediately intervene when I saw anyone being bullied. As I began to understand how widespread it was, I found myself beginning to seek out the perpetrators in an effort to stop them before they could even think of doing it. I was relentless. I was on a mission. At one point, a colleague of mine told me to give it a rest and let the kids work it out themselves. I didn't know what to think. Was he serious? Had he been one of those bullies during his school years? Regardless of what any other teacher did or didn't do, I didn't let it stop me. I had a purpose, and if I could make a difference in just one child's life, it would all be worth it.

Although I never stopped addressing the issue, I noticed over time how most of my colleagues acted as if it wasn't their job to get involved. As crazy as that sounds to me now, I think they were just chicken and didn't want to deal with confrontation from the parents of either group of kids—those who were bullying or those who were being bullied. It angered me to no end.

After a time, I left the teaching field to become a writer; in a way, I guess I was paying homage to those who came before me and helped me as a child. They will never know, but each one of those people, both real and imaginary, helped pull me through some of my darkest days.

It seems weird to say, but although the first half of my life was incredibly painful, I still wouldn't trade it because the second half of my life has been so great. In many ways, I think the bullying taught me to be strong and resilient, and I learned quickly how to depend on myself. Although they were valuable lessons, they certainly didn't come without a price tag—one that almost became too steep to pay.

Now that I have my own children and a healthy, happy marriage to a wonderful man, I am happier than I ever thought possible, probably because I had never really known what happiness was before. In many ways, I am reliving my childhood through my children and enjoying every minute of it. We have chosen to homeschool our children so we don't have to worry about things like bullying in their lives and they have healthy, respectful relationships with other children who are mostly homeschooled, too—the kinds of relationships that, in my opinion, too many children are deprived of.

About the Author

Patricia Brown is the pseudonym of an educator who homeschools her children. Having experienced bullying as a youth and as a youth advocate, she is now the caring mother of three youngsters. From her perspective, authority figures have a responsibility to prevent bullying. Her advice to those who are being bullied is to find something they are passionate about and use that as an outlet, whether it be reading (as it was for her), writing, running, crafting, or whatever. She recommends that they find something they enjoy that is just theirs so they can get lost in it for a while and take a break from the pain.

From Victim to Expert

By Nicole Mayo

"Knowing what's right doesn't mean much
unless you do what's right."
—Theodore Roosevelt, Former President

When I was asked to compose a piece about my own experiences of bullying and how that led to a successful career studying the lasting impact of bullying into adulthood, I hit my first real bout of writer's block in a decade-long profession. I found myself hard-pressed to tackle such a personal subject. Although I have built a career around industrial/organizational psychology and teaching others about occupational hazards such as workplace bullying, I found myself writing, re-writing, and writing again, never quite happy with how the words flowed when it came time to tell my own story. Finally, I realized the issue: it was difficult to put my experience into words because my story starts out from the perspective of a victim, but that's not how it ends.

I distinctly remember my kindergarten teacher referring to me as a social butterfly (and thinking it would be pretty darn awesome to *be* a butterfly). I remember how hard second grade was when my two best friends at school moved away. And by third grade, I recall suddenly becoming *that* kid. You know—the one who sticks out like a sore thumb. Suddenly, I found myself diagnosed with severe asthma, which limited my ability to participate in recess and gym class, and before long I was the kid sitting on the sidelines, watching the rest of the class playing. Since that was the only chance we were given to socialize, I soon fell out of the tight-knit social group in the small private school I attended.

By fourth grade, I wore glasses, was a voracious reader and a known regular at my local library, and excelled at schoolwork. My asthma had kept me from most physical activity, and I had also turned into the fat kid. So let's recap—I was the fat, four-eyed bookworm girl constantly disrupting class with my asthma attacks and being shuffled off to the nurse's office. Top it off with over two years of rarely being given a chance to socialize, and frankly, I'm shocked it wasn't worse.

Kids can be vicious assholes, and this is readily apparent as early as the toddler years. Research even supports a distinct difference in the ways in which boys and girls bully. Boys tend to engage in physical aggression, intimidating and dominating in a direct attempt to defend and improve their social standing. Their attacks are targeted and purposeful; their victim is still allowed to have his or her social group so long as everyone knows their place in the pack.

But girls—*girls* engage in relational aggression, and their tactics are much more insidious. Girls will directly attack any relationship they feel is supporting their victim, using manipulation to break up subgroups and turn the entire social unit against the victim. Once the dominant young lady decides you're out, you're in total social isolation. I still remember the day I realized that I had no friends.

It started with little things, minor exclusions. One girl brought mechanical pencils and slap bracelets (hello, early '90s) to literally every kid in the class except me. I watched my whole class exchange birthday party invitations for an entire year—while I didn't receive a single one. I remember the very last birthday party I threw, where the two most popular girls in my class (who also ruled my Girl Scout troop, but that's another story) were the only people to show up— and they ignored me the whole time. They even stood next to my desk at school on Monday morning, announcing to the class in loud voices that they only went because their parents made them and expounding on how lucky everyone else was to not have had to go.

Eventually, the social exclusion turned to active teasing, and finally to physical abuse. Boys are far more likely to just get into an out-and-out brawl, while girls are far more cunning when it comes to orchestrating physical attacks. A group of boys will use subtle forms of intimidation at school, then corner a victim out of sight of adults and quickly escalate to punches and beatings. A group of girls will engage in hair pulling, pinching, tripping, and other tactics designed to embarrass the victim whenever the teacher's back is turned.

One of the few days I felt physically able to participate in games at recess, I was tripped by one of the bullies' ringleaders, face-planted on the concrete blacktop, and wound up with hairline fractures in three fingers. Another day, I was doing cartwheels with the few kids from other classes in the grassy area of the courtyard. I overheard the bullies talking, egging each other on to "Do it!" as they got closer, and braced myself to ignore another onslaught of insults. They waited until I was upside down, feet in the air, and body slammed me to the ground.

The teachers were so enamored with the socially outgoing, eye-batting popular girls that I was lectured for the remainder of the day about how irresponsible I was for injuring the girl who shoved me. She scraped her knee and cried giant crocodile tears for the next several hours. I wasn't allowed to call home, and by the time school was dismissed, my neck was visibly swollen and I couldn't turn my head. I spent the night in the ER having my neck x-rayed and was told I was a drama queen for wearing a soft neck brace to school for the next week. I still can't turn my head to the left without pain, more than a quarter of a century later.

Fortunately, in fifth grade I was switched to public school and finally had the opportunity to develop deep friendships that have lasted into adulthood. But the small private school I had attended was failing, and several of the children from my early years also switched to the same public school. Even more of my former classmates showed up in middle school, and the entire gang was there by high school. They hadn't forgotten that early childhood training, and though the physical abuse stopped, the rumor spreading and friendship sabotaging escalated at an astronomical rate.

My freshman year of high school began in a Denver public school the semester immediately following the massacre shooting at Columbine High School in Jefferson County, Colorado. The second day of school, I was exchanging my giant stack of books for my lunch bag when my locker was slammed shut in front of me and a girl I had never seen before informed me that she was going to kill me so she didn't have to look at my fat face all year long. I was terrified and went straight to the school counselor. He immediately asked me, "What did you do to provoke this?"

I don't remember the name of that counselor, but he helped define who I was to become. In that moment, I went from terrified, depressed, and suicidal to absolutely livid. I instantly knew that this attitude from the authority figures who were supposed to protect victims was the real problem with the bullying cycle. For the first time in my goodie-two-shoes, ultra-passive life, I yelled at an adult. I will never forget the look on his face when I told him that that type of attitude was what led bullying victims to snap and attack back. I left and walked home.

That comment, made in the heat of the moment and from a mindset of sheer terror, really landed me in hot water. I was asked to pore through yearbooks and identify the bully, who was asked to give me a forced apology in the office of the same counselor who would remain convinced that I was the problem. I was sent to therapy, and the wonderful counselor I was placed with helped me channel my anger and utilize wonderful coping skills to stand up to the bullying and build wonderful friendships that have continued to this day.

At the beginning of my sophomore year, I transferred to an online program for gifted students and soon moved on to college. I built wonderful friendships and working relationships, and I met and fell in love with my husband. I also suffered through a series of incredibly abusive bosses as I worked my way through school and was baffled by the in-crowd, cliquish behavior in the department of my university. Over the years, I became more and more puzzled by the fact that I was still seeing so much bullying between adults—and even among psychologists and therapists!

I began working on a masters' degree in school counseling with the intention of helping bullied children find peace with their experiences, and I found myself absolutely fascinated by the concept of adult bullying. I switched majors to industrial/organizational psychology and began to delve deeply into the effects of bullying on adults. What I have found so far in my career is both incredibly surprising and incredibly—not.

The effects of childhood bullying have a profound effect on the psyche and well-being of the victim, and these patterns of behavior have the potential to extend into adulthood. While childhood bullies appear to come out unscathed, their victims are at a significantly increased risk of poor psychosocial and economic functioning as adults, regardless of whether they also went on to engage in bullying themselves. The damaging effects of childhood bullying on self-esteem are thought to explain the tendency of victims to have lower employment rates and below-average pay, which leaves them at risk for decreased psychosocial functioning across the lifespan. That's right—being bullied as a child puts the victim at risk for lifelong depression, anxiety, and poverty, and that is a vicious cycle to try to break out of.

Victims of childhood bullying spanning more than three years display decreased decision-making capabilities, reduced use of coping mechanisms, lowered sense of control, and increased levels of emotional sensitivity, anger, and fear. Exposure to childhood bullying has also been linked to daily heavy smoking, while engaging in bullying as a child is strongly linked to the development of illicit substance abuse addictions. Even witnessing bullying behaviors can lead to significant increases in psychological distress, particularly for witnesses who have also been the target of bullying themselves.

The profound effects of bullying on adults clearly demonstrate that this is not a problem left behind on the playgrounds of childhood. In the workplace, adults use verbal aggression to harm the professional reputation of others, using deceptive tactics and denying resources to intentionally set victims up for failure at a given task so that they can be hung out to dry as the weakest link dragging the work team down. This workplace isolation is often perceived by witnesses as one of the harshest things that can be done to a colleague, and yet many individuals are so thankful to have a job in the current economy that they cannot bring themselves to report bullying out of fear of retaliation.

More often than not, the presence of bullying in the workplace creates a strong grouping effect. The social strata become increasingly separated, the productivity of the victim and the entire work team tanks, and the victim spirals into bouts of depression, anxiety, and sleep disturbances that leave him or her exhausted and physically ill. The lower the victim's self-esteem falls, the more likely he or she is to passively accept the bullying behavior and internalize the message that something is wrong with *him or her*, not the bully. The victim may take an increased number of sick days in an effort to cope and frequently leaves his or her position altogether as a direct result of bullying.

All of this makes sense to me—except for the very important question of *why* bullies act the way they do. Having become a confident and socially engaged individual who has long since processed the trauma of my own bullying, I decided that the best way to fully answer this question was to track down and contact my own bullies. Some are just nameless faces lost in distant memory. But some stuck out sufficiently to track down, and many were surprisingly willing to talk about their bullying behaviors.

The girl in third grade who started the classroom trend of excluding me? She said she was punished every time she brought home a grade that wasn't the top of the class. Guess who tended to have that honor? I mean, really, I had absolutely nothing to do but study during my downtime—I had no friends to distract me. The two girls who ruled the Girl Scout troop and ostracized me at my own party? One is struggling with addiction, and the other is a successful public speaker. They both said they only did that because one of the other girls told them to, and they couldn't even remember who.

Interestingly, one of the worst bullies who led the relational aggression tactics against me in high school was a close friend of mine in middle school. She also added me on Facebook a few years back, and when I asked her at the time if she remembered how we parted ways, she didn't even recall that she had led a systematic attack on my friendships and egged on the girl who had threatened to kill me. After a few years of "liking" each other's statuses, I floated the question to her again. This time, she confessed that the first week of high school, she had developed a crush on one of the boys from that small private school where it all began, and they had actually been working together with the goal of getting me to transfer or commit suicide.

Let's stop and talk about that. The levels of depression and anxiety that can come about as a direct result of bullying are absolutely crippling. Heartbreakingly, suicide rates for bullying victims of all ages are approximately nine times higher than for those who aren't bullied. You read that right—an individual who is bullied is *nine times* more likely to consider suicide as a means of escape. That's on top of the drastically reduced self-esteem and increased rates of depression, anxiety, PTSD, and alcohol and substance abuse.

Now let's talk about how experiencing bullying has made me a more successful person than I ever would have been before. Before I could drive a car, I knew what rock-bottom felt like, and I survived. I not only survived, I *thrived*—by learning how *not* to treat people. Those school-yard lessons have made me a compassionate, caring, empathetic, and mindful person, and those skills have made me a far more successful leader, partner, and mother than I ever would have been had I lived a candy-coated perfect life. Most importantly, those experiences gave me the passion to tackle bullying as a pervasive and lifelong social phenomenon.

While there are laws preventing an individual's employment from being affected by membership in a protected class, American workers currently have no legal protection from the deliberate use of aggressive bullying tactics to demean and harm the victim's psyche, so long as the victim is able to maintain his or her employment status. The limited research conducted on targeting bullying interventions has shown that simply setting anti-bullying policies is just the first step in solving workplace bullying, and yet interventions solely targeting victims or designed to change workplace culture as a whole have mixed results at best and generally appear to be ineffective.

Children look to the adults in their lives to teach them the tools needed to stand up against bullying, and as a society we falsely assume that adults possess those skills. The next generation of bullying interventions must approach bullying from a holistic perspective: teaching bullies strategies for achieving their goals that do not involve targeting others, empowering victims with the coping skills needed to stand their ground, calling on witnesses to actively join the fight against bullying culture, and actively discouraging the use of the Internet's anonymity to attack others.

Bullying is a group phenomenon that, once sparked, spreads like wildfire through a forest. The only way to stop it is to break the pattern of slow burn and teach adults the appropriate skills so they can plant the seeds of conscientiousness, kindness, and empathy in the next generation in order to ensure that they remain free of the lifelong burdens of bullying. The ultimate goal of my career is to help shift the way society as a whole thinks about bullying and to discover effective and targeted anti-bullying intervention methods for all age groups that incorporate coping skills for the victim and that teach the bully empathy, mindfulness, and positive strategies for achieving goals.

I was a victim. I was isolated. I was bullied. I stood up. I spoke out. I will not hide. I will not stand idle. I will prevail, and so will you.

About the Author

Nicole Mayo has a master's degree in industrial/organizational psychology, a field that studies how people behave at work. Within this discipline, she further specializes in the analysis of occupational health and wellness, exploring factors that impact the mental, emotional, and physical well-being of workers. Even more specifically, she studies factors at work that lead to increased levels of employee stress and how stress affects individuals in the workplace. Over the years, she has come to realize that the leading cause of employee stress is bullying and has spent the past five years attempting to get to the bottom of workplace bullying.

Part III: Friendship

"When we honestly ask ourselves which
person in our lives means the most to us, we
often find that it is those who, instead of
giving advice, solutions, or cures, have chosen
rather to share our pain and touch our
wounds with a warm and tender hand."
—Henri J. M. Nouwen, Author

Bringing Down the Bullies

By Shruti Fatehpuria

> "Each friend represents a world in us, a world
> possibly not born until they arrive, and it is
> only by this meeting that a new world is
> born."
> —Anais Nin, Author

I vividly recall the day when I entered my new school in the ninth standard. I was a little skeptical of going to a new school and leaving my old friends behind. However, when I stepped inside the school, I was warmly welcomed and made new friends instantly.

I laughed at my ridiculous nightmares of being made fun of and bullied because I ended up finding people to be really sweet. However, there was a girl in my class who never seemed to speak much. I once asked others what was wrong with her, and they told her to come to our table to "show me."

She was literally trembling as she approached our table. Her eyes glistened with what looked like tears, and she stuttered and pleaded to be left alone. All my so-called "good friends" erupted in laughter and told her to at least "man up" in front of the new girl. I couldn't understand what was amiss and, not feeling good about the situation, asked everyone to stop.

Obviously, my gesture didn't sit well with my new friends, who told me that this was how things rolled. I moved closer to the girl and sat beside her. I saw that she was still trembling and asked her to calm down. She broke down in an uncontrollable pool of tears. I was shocked to find so much pain inside her.

"Don't do this to me. Tell me, what is the plan? I can't bear it any longer. Tell me what you want me to do, and I will do it. Please do not play with me," she said, stuttering and crying all the while. I couldn't understand what she meant, and I sat there clueless. I offered her a drink of water and tried to comfort her. The more I tried to comfort her, the more she trembled. I couldn't understand what was wrong or why she was so scared.

I had never seen someone so petrified before. For an instant, I wondered if I should leave her alone and give her some time to recover; however, my instincts told me to stay there with her. I lost count of how long I was sitting there, but slowly her sobs started ebbing away.

Finally, after what seemed like thirty minutes or so, she looked up at me with fear in her eyes and stammered, "You aren't going to make a video of the whole crying scene, are you?"

I was baffled beyond words and said, "Why would I?!" To this, she gave a joyless laugh and said because that was what everyone did, that was what was in her destiny, and that was why she was born. I couldn't believe all of it, and I asked her to tell me the whole story.

She was too scared, but somehow she sensed my genuine concern for her, and we both went to the cafeteria, where she took me to one forlorn corner that was marked "Abandoned." I asked her why this chair and she quietly replied, "It is *my* bench."

"It was two years back when I entered this school. I used to be a very bubbly child, and I brimmed with confidence. I made friends instantly, and people were really happy to be around me. It wasn't until the first month that I realized that their love and friendliness was all a pretense. They had noted every single detail about me and even made a spoof film of me. I was mortified, and everyone was ridiculing me. They had embarrassing pictures of me posted in the video. This destroyed my confidence, and I was asked not to open my mouth or else they said they would circulate the video further. I cried and they filmed that, too. I was so devastated that I lost all my confidence. Every day has been a struggle since then. When my teacher asked me about the sudden change in behavior, I shared the whole incident. The teacher rebuked the students, which further enraged them. This is why the whole class has shunned me. Every day at school is like time spent in hell. I tried talking to my parents, but they just think it is a passing phase."

After she finished her story, she broke down completely. I knew that it was time to do something, so I asked her not to give up. The so-called friends I had made were nothing short of devils. They needed to learn a lesson because *bullying someone is not a joke.* They didn't just bully this girl—they made her lifeless and devoid of feelings. She was a living skeleton. I decided I had to do something. But I needed the right opportunity.

It's said that fortune favors the brave. Soon my English teacher announced a project where we were supposed to highlight an issue of prime importance with a case study. I knew exactly what I needed to do. It wouldn't be easy, but it would be worth it. I teamed with the bullied girl to make a very short film about her life—the way she used to be cheerful and the whole sequence of how a spoof film was made and the rejection she faced. Finally, there was a scene that showed how she was suffering currently. However, the video didn't end with a depressing message. It showed karma smiling at the back. Finally, the girl rose to the stage, smiled, wiped away her tears, and spoke fearlessly about why every bullied person should stand up to bullying because if you don't, the chain reaction never stops. We ended with this line in our presentation:

"Twenty-five years down the line, karma smiles at the sight of a new victim . . . the daughter of the culprit now turns victim. The scoreboard reads 1–1."

It was enough to make the class realize that their deeds were not going to be unpunished. I stood in front of the class and thanked Neha, the girl who was bullied, for helping me create a project I resonated so strongly with. We are now best friends. The whole class apologized to her, and the teacher also realized the severity of the situation. This same girl currently works at a leading multinational company. In her time off, she works with a charitable organization to assist victims of bullying and other oppression because, she tells me, all it takes is one helping hand!

Say no to bullying and remember: karma always bites back!

About the Author

In a world where almost everyone is striving to stand out by outdoing others, Shruti Fatehpuria aims at merely finding her own place in the crowd. A software engineer by education, she made the choice to quit the suffocating clutches of the corporate world and embrace the comfort of pen and paper.

Alone

By Camille B.

"Friendship is born at that moment when one
man says to another: 'What! You too? I
thought that no one but myself …'"
—C. S. Lewis, Author

"Look, I think I found your classroom. Is this the correct classroom?" asked my mother.

I stepped up to the door and looked up at the nameplate above the window. There, clear as day, was written "7A." The same room assignment printed on my student permit. Correct, then.

Right then and there, my emotions assaulted me, as they would assault anyone who had just transferred to both a new school and a new home. Change is daunting to anyone, and perhaps it would be especially so for a shy twelve-year-old who had just had both her daily environments changed drastically.

Fear. Curiosity. Excitement.

"I see that a lot of your classmates are there already. Why don't you go in?" my mother encouraged.

"Don't worry, we'll be here for awhile if ever you need us," my father chimed in.

So I opened the door, and twenty or so other adolescent heads turned toward me. Their eyes spoke their recognition at what I was. *New student.*

I quickly found a place near the back of the room and kept quiet.

The rest of the day passed uneventfully, as did the entire next month or so. It was the usual classroom: the veterans used this time to catch up with their peers, while the new kids used the time to prove themselves worthy of attention and friendship.

And, much faster than I thought anyone could, they did. Left and right, my fellow new kids were making friends rapidly, becoming part of their own cliques and groups. They began to become indistinguishable from the old-timers as they lost the "new kid" vibe.

As for me, I stayed friendless. For many weeks, I had no one to hang out with at recess, and no one to talk to but the library books at lunch. To some extent, I was content with this arrangement. I have never been a very social person, and I valued silence. I would have been completely okay with the solitude had it not been that the whispers were gaining traction and my classmates' treatment of me was growing fouler day by day.

To this day, I don't know how it started. I don't know what they saw in me that was so undesirable or disgusting, but they made it evident to me, every day, that they did. No one would touch anything I had touched, and people would refuse to sit next to me at gatherings or even in the classroom. The hallway to my classroom would clear of people whenever I passed, and when they couldn't clear out, they would stick to the walls as though I were a walking epidemic. My classmates would insult me and call me names whenever they could ("Who are your group mates?" "Oh, just Bryan, Valerie, and, unfortunately, The Idiot . . .") and would quickly ignore anything I tried to contribute to group discussion, despite the fact that I did well in class.

No one ever spoke to me or wanted to be near me. No one listened to me. No one respected me, and they went to great lengths to show me that. Every day I was a source of entertainment, and hour upon hour they waited for me to fail or step out of the norm, like vultures over carrion, so they could make my failure the talk of the day. My suffering was their delight, and they delighted in violating my things and humiliating me.

People whispered and laughed behind my back when they thought I couldn't hear them. But I could, and it hurt. The constant ridicule and contempt began to weigh heavily on me and seriously impact my self-esteem, of which there wasn't much in the first place. I was asking myself, every second of every day, "What is wrong with me?" "Why are they doing this?" When I could not answer any of the endless streams of questions I threw at myself, I became ever more confused and lost. Every day, I struggled to get out of bed because I knew that suffering was in store. All day at school, I carefully watched my actions and tried to keep myself in check, but to no avail, despite it heavily weighing me down emotionally and mentally. At the end of every day, I would stay silent for the entire trip home and crash on the couch immediately upon coming home, crying more often than not.

With every day, the situation seemed to grow worse and worse. From the confines of my class, the trend of treating me badly began to spread to the other classes until it grew harder and harder to find someplace I could breathe.

Every day I asked myself the same questions, and every day I failed to answer them. Life went on. My cycle of endless solitude continued, and the other students continued to treat me as subhuman. Deeper and deeper I sank, deteriorating emotionally, until I finally found an oasis that was not a mirage like the rest.

I applied, and got accepted, to the school paper. For the first time in many weeks, I found a place where I was not cast off at every opportunity. I found a place where I could speak and my voice would be heard, a place where I didn't have to keep myself in check constantly and could be myself, a place where I was with my own.

It was a family and always has been. In the school paper, I found the kin I could not find elsewhere: the quiet ones, the eccentrics, and most importantly, the accepting ones. Here I found the strength to defy my own descent and deterioration, and to ignore the subhuman treatment.

Of course, I made friends. Being of the same shy, quiet, socially inept feather, it took some time, but it developed well and blossomed. At first, we were content, every time we gathered, with knowing that we were among kin: there would be no ridicule there, no weights. We could be ourselves. Then slowly, we started speaking to each other. We shared our stories, our experiences, our (unsurprisingly numerous) common interests, and our views.

This slow but steady process culminated at lunchtime one day. Two of my friends (at that point, I was already very much beginning to think of them as friends) were at one table, and I was at the opposite table, alone. We exchanged some words and cracked some jokes across tables, but the truth at that time was apparent: they were at their table, I was at mine, and I was alone. This did not go unnoticed by them.

After a lull in the conversation, my two friends awkwardly asked me, "Hey . . . do you want to sit at our table? We happen to have two seats free, and we'd like you to occupy one." Of course, I was happy to oblige. To this day, those two are still very firmly in my circle of friends, which has since grown considerably.

It's easy to underestimate the weight of this event. After all, lunchtime table arrangements may be perceived as pitifully trivial. However, life is full of real-life symbolism—the active everyday kind, not just the passive kind we see in books—because humans do not only communicate verbally. Perhaps this phenomenon is even more apparent in socially awkward teenagers, who are not always the best at expressing themselves. That simple transfer from one table to another meant acceptance to me, long thirsted for but never truly attained until that moment. My days of solitude were over.

In the midst of all this, I was very surprised during one otherwise unremarkable Wednesday morning to note something rather beautiful: I was looking forward to school again. I was beginning to see beyond my classmates' treatment of me, right to the things I actually enjoy no matter what. Learning, reading, writing, and the discussions with my newfound friends from the school paper empowered me and gave me the strength to carry on.

With this strength, I began to change. The self-esteem I sorely lacked was beginning to return, and I began to start to truly hold my own against those who attacked me emotionally. In essence, I began to learn to become the person I am within the closed doors of the meetings of the school paper *outside* those closed doors, too. It was a very slow process, just like how I found my friends, and myself. This slow process is still ongoing, but it is also very, very sure.

I don't fully know how I earned the respect of some of my classmates, but quite a few of them began treating me better toward the end of the year, and some even came up to me to apologize. In retrospect, it is important to note that in every bullying situation, not all of those who treat you badly wish to do so or are actually bullies beyond skin-deep. The vast majority are just acting out of peer pressure. They see you suffer, and they recognize this, and so you gain their respect.

The rest, as they say, is history. Our group of friends has continued to grow, although by our nature it has never been especially large. We—as a group, not just myself—continued to gain the respect of not only our bullies but also the general student populace as they began to accept our eccentricities and recognize that we have talents of our own.

I was eventually promoted to Associate Editor, where I was tasked with trying to tame the close-knit roughhouse that our school paper has become—mostly failing, because more often than not, I was less than responsible and quite a few times an instigator. My deep love for the sciences blossomed after being held back.

The ordeal that was seventh grade is not the last emotional roller coaster I went through, and I suspect that as a human being, there will be quite a few more before my last. There is a crucial difference, however: the subsequent ones I faced with the excellent, not-infallible but always-there support system made up of friends and family. Currently, I am a graduating student, and that was five years ago. Hopefully, I have grown much since then.

On the last day of our last high school English class, our teacher, who had been there to watch us since fateful seventh grade, was reminiscing on how we had been and marveling at who we are now as graduating students.

Out of the blue, my teacher exclaimed, clearly referring to me, "And you! When you were in seventh grade, you were the quiet, seemingly angry girl at the back of the classroom, trying so very hard to find your place! Look at how you've changed!"

Out of curiosity, I asked. "How am I now?"

And to that she responded, evidently proud, "Like seventh grade never happened."

About the Author

Camille B. is a freelance writer who grew up in the Philippines. She enjoys helping others.

"The best way to not feel hopeless is to get up
and do something. Don't wait for good things
to happen to you. If you go out and make
some good things happen, you will fill the
world with hope, you will fill yourself with
hope."

—President Barack Obama, World Leader

The Wallflower

By Bhavya Kaushik

"Not for ourselves alone are we born."

—Cicero, Philosopher

When I was a kid, my mother told me to beware of fire—that it can burn you irrevocably and leave scars on your skin. I listened to her and kept my distance from it. But she never warned me about the flames that people carry inside themselves. I got lost, and I got burned—terribly, piece by piece, until there was nothing left of me. I was burned to ashes, not by physical fire but by the inner flames of certain people.

I have always been a geek and was often addressed by the term "dork" or "that skinny kid" in high school. My grades were phenomenal—I never got anything lower than an A+ during the entire course of my high school. But I never had many friends, because in order to make friends you have to talk to people, and I have never been very good at expressing myself. I was an introvert, a listener, a daydreamer, a vagabond lost in my own journey. I was the wallflower about whose existence nobody cared.

As I was growing up, I realized that life is unfair and not all your dreams can come true. When my own classmates started bullying me for no apparent reason, I realized that not everything in this world is our choice. When the people whom I used to consider my friends joined the bullies club and started picking on me, I realized that people can change and can leave you in a heartbeat. When I fell in love and got rejected, I realized that some people can only stay in your heart, not in your life. But what I didn't realize was that, with every rejection, my heart was breaking into pieces. I didn't realize that every time my own friends with whom I used to play hide-and-seek in kindergarten were picking on me or calling me names, my self-esteem was plummeting. It dropped so low that I forgot I had ever been content.

It all started during that unforgettable summer when one of my classmates asked me to complete an assignment for him. I didn't find the idea appealing—the teacher wanted to read his opinion, not mine—so I declined the offer. He didn't say anything at that moment, but I realized he was furious when I found both of my bicycle tires punctured at the end of class. I walked home that day and found him standing near my street. He didn't say anything. He just walked by, looking at me as if he would kill me at any moment. I didn't know what to do—I was upset and terrified, but there was nothing I could do. After all, I was a lost child, and I had no voice. I was the wallflower.

I thought that things would get better in time, but they didn't. Gradually, my classmates started making fun of me. It started with one person, but soon I found the entire class—the entire school—standing on the other side of the cliff. They would call me by various names and pass abusive notes to me for no reason at all. Strangers pushed me in the hallways and humiliated me in front of everyone.

There was no reason at all for their behavior—except, of course, that I was an easy target and wasn't brave enough to raise my voice.

Initially, I thought it would go away, that it was just a phase and wouldn't last forever, but I was wrong. I was doomed to live with it for the rest of high school. People called me many names, but I guess the most prominent one was "pan face." I tried to build a wall around my heart that would prevent it from breaking in pieces, but I couldn't.

Their words hurt more than their actions ever did. I started to question myself every day. The trail of questions was endless, from "Do I really look that bad?" to "Am I such a bad person?" and from "What can I do to make it stop?" to "What is the reason for my existence?".

I found it hard to enter a room full of people. My sense of self-worth and confidence vanished into nothingness. I would eat lunch alone every day, sit alone every day. I was left with no friends, no shelter, no light to guide my way home. I was caught in a whirlpool of self-destruction, and there was no one left to save me.

One day, I found a note on my desk that read, "This world would be a better place without you!" I guess that note triggered the idea of self-destruction in my mind. I never thought I would do it until I found myself holding a blade, cutting my own skin.

I started to self-harm because I wanted to be in control. I was living in a world where I felt I couldn't control a thing. I couldn't stop people from leaving me forever. I couldn't stop them from bullying me or calling me names. I couldn't even stop my thoughts in my own head. In a world full of uncertainties, there was only one thing that I was able to control. Cutting. I knew where to cut and I knew how to cut. I knew when to stop. Ironically, cutting was the one thing that made me feel happy. It made me take control of my life. Or at least I thought so.

I didn't cut myself every day. It wasn't a daily chore or a hobby. I would cut whenever depression would start taking a toll on me. On one of the last days of high school, I had a bad fight with someone. I walked straight to the bathroom, rolled up my sleeves, and cut myself with a razor blade. I didn't know then that it would be my last time.

I was familiar with self-harming, but something was different that day. Instead of cutting my upper skin, I made a deep cut in my vein. Blood started to ooze out of my wrist, and it didn't stop. I tried to cover it with a Band-Aid, but the dam had broken. When I knew I couldn't stop the blood, I put a cloth over the wound to cover the bleeding and called my parents.

I don't remember exactly what happened afterward since I lost consciousness. I woke up after a while in a hospital bed. I didn't know how I got there or who had brought me. But I knew I was alive. And that feeling was life changing. I was overwhelmingly happy that I was alive. For a moment, I thought I could do anything. I believed I could fly. And so I did.

I took control of my life after that near-death experience. I saw my parents, and I realized how much they had always loved me. I saw my own reflection in the mirror and realized that I don't need anyone else to make me feel happy. I could dance *my* way, on my own.

I have always been a one-man army, and it was my time to shine. I became the writer of my own life and stopped listening to what other people said about me. After all, it was my life, not theirs. I always wanted to be a writer, but my insecurities wouldn't allow me to be so vulnerable and raw. But I was a whole new person, so I penned a novel about my past.

The novel was published and did so well that it was declared a national bestseller. With every step I took, I regained a small part of my self-esteem. I was a brand-new me with an astonishing amount of confidence.

I was successful. I was living my dreams, but something was still missing. I found my last piece when I met a reader of my book who came up to me during a book-signing event and shared with me her entire story. She told me about how she used to self-harm and was close to committing suicide. When she read my book, she said, it changed her life. She said she was alive because of me.

Her words mended my broken heart back into a whole, well-functioning organ. It was healed. My sense of self-esteem was replenished.

I never cut myself after that incident. Some of my scars are gone, but some are still with me, and I wear them courageously like battle wounds. Some scars can really change your life. They changed mine, at least.

I'm happy now, more than ever. It took me a long time to realize that I don't need the entire world to define my existence. I exist. I exist, and that is more than enough for me.

I'm not a wallflower anymore. The flower has fallen from the wall. The flower is replanted in firm ground, and growing strong.

About the Author

With a master's degree in computer science, Bhavya Kaushik believes that versatility is the key to unlock every door of our aspirations. Author of a best-selling novel, he is in pursuit of his unwavering passion to talk about things that touch our soul and leave an everlasting impression. He is on a quest to seek answers to the questions that have always kept him awake at night. He is the author of his own journey.

Training Bras and Torture

By Diana Eastman

"It takes courage to grow up and become who
you really are."

—e. e. Cummings, Poet

I was thirteen and had no idea why my body was freaking out on me. I would have to sneak a razor to shave my legs because my mom insisted I used Nair, the hair-removal cream that literally made me gag. I was terrified when I got my period and was certain I would be flat chested forever. Thirteen-year-olds have it rough.

It was during this awkward time that I began to wear a bra, although looking back now, I didn't even need one. I had two bras that my mom bought for me; one was a training bra and the other was a padded bra. Some days I would wear my regular bra, accentuating my flatness, and other days I'd wear my padded bra and suddenly, va-va-voom, I felt like a Victoria's Secret model.

Looking back, I'm sure it looked a little weird for me to come to school on Monday flat as a pancake and Tuesday as a B cup. But what did I know? I was thirteen, and I was wearing a bra. I even stretched out the shoulders of my shirts so that my bra straps would show and everyone who walked by would clearly see that I was wearing a bra. Thankfully, my mom put an end to that trashy fashion trend right away.

For some reason, Erica, who had the body of a sixteen-year-old at this point, didn't like the variations in my chest size. She noticed that sometimes I was flat and sometimes there was a little something there, and for some reason she didn't like it. And so the torture began.

It started with "loud enough for me to hear" comments directed at me from the back of the classroom about how "she don't even need a bra!" Of course, the table of busty girls sitting around Erica would break out in hyena-like laughter, and I'd pretend I didn't hear it. I thought if I ignored it, she would stop. Not so much.

There were a few times when we were in the classroom before the teacher got there, and Erica would draw an artistic rendition of me, never forgetting the pudgy belly I was so self-conscious about or the fluctuating size of my chest. Then I tried the "if you can't beat 'em, join 'em" technique and encouraged her to add my braces and out-of-style shoes to the drawing. Bad idea. She accused me of "trying to be funny" and "having an attitude with her," which only escalated things further.

One morning before class, some girl I didn't know came up and handed me a tissue. Then someone else came up and did the same thing. In first period, one of the cutest guys in school handed me a tissue but didn't say a word. I didn't realize what was going on until third period, when I had tissues coming out of everywhere. Erica met me in the hall with a box of tissues and said, "I thought you could use these to put in your bra tomorrow." It was like a scene from a movie. I felt as though the halls were silent and everyone was looking at me.

Erica's face was intimidating, and she was begging me to say something she didn't like. I knew she wouldn't hesitate to knock me out, so I stayed quiet and still. I took the box and tried to stop my hands from shaking. She broke out in a scary heckle and walked away from me, and I realized I wasn't breathing. I threw the box of tissues out and did everything in my power not to cry.

I wore big, baggy sweatshirts after that, even as the hot Florida summers approached. For some reason, she didn't bother me after that; she probably moved on to some other self-conscious teenager who was just trying to get through being thirteen.

I'm lucky that my situation never escalated to anything physical, but it didn't make the embarrassment or fear any less real. I actually sat in front of Erica a few years later in high school, and she was as nice as could be. I couldn't figure out whether it was because she remembered and was sorry or whether she had tormented so many people that year that she really didn't even remember me. Either way, I forgave her and we were civil for the rest of the year.

Because this happened to me in middle school, I was always hyperaware of anyone whom I felt was being picked on or embarrassed by other classmates. Although I was never brave enough to stand up to the bully, I would go out of my way to befriend the victim, to sit with her when nobody else would and listen to her story when everyone else ignored her. I wished someone had come up to me and said, "Hey, they're pathetic—don't worry about it. Do you want to be in our study group?" I didn't have that person in my life, so I made it a point to be that person for others.

Bullying is not "what kids do." It is not okay, safe, productive, or acceptable. It is my hope that kids who have been through this situation can seek out a friend, teacher, or family member and let them know what is going on. It's also my hope that kids will be brave enough to stand up for their peers, even if they're the only one standing.

About the Author

Diana Eastman graduated from the University of Central Florida with a degree in Communications. She works as a freelance writer and lives in Orlando, Florida.

Part V: Outside Help

"One of the greatest barriers to connection is the cultural importance we place on 'going it alone.' Somehow we've come to equate success with not needing anymore. Many of us are willing to extend a helping hand, but we're very reluctant to reach out for help when we need it ourselves. It's as if we've divided the world into 'those who offer help' and 'those who need help.' The truth is we are both."

—Brené Brown, Author

On the Roadside

By William Anderson

"Childhood should be carefree, playing in the
sun; not living a nightmare in the darkness of
the soul."

—Dave Pelzer, Author

When Alex was fifteen, his parents put him and his three younger sisters into their van, drove to the Iowa–Missouri border, opened the sliding door, and pushed them out. The parents then turned the van around and drove away.

Alex and his sisters walked along a dirt road for miles until they became exhausted. Days later, the children were rescued by the police and placed into the custody of Children's Division. After several temporary placements, Alex was transferred to a children's home.

Alex didn't speak for six months. His abusive father had been so violent that Alex had learned not to say a word in order to be invisible. He didn't talk to his therapists, house managers, psychiatrist, state social worker, or the other children. Sometimes the kids tried to start fights with him, but Alex didn't take the bait. He stayed silent.

Months later, as he began to trust a therapist, he said a few words to her. He was testing her ability to be accepting and trustworthy. As their relationship developed, Alex started to reveal his high level of intelligence and sense of humor. After a year, the staff introduced Alex to the board of directors, and he captivated them one by one as he gave them tours of the home.

The most difficult part of Alex's transition was coming out. For the most part, he only revealed his secret to his therapist because he was afraid the kids might pick fights with him. As a result of opening up, Alex began to find self-confidence. Instead of having to worry about the things no child should ever have to, Alex was given a second chance. Alex excelled at the school on the children's home campus. Eventually, he graduated and found a home worthy of having him.

One person can make a difference in the life of another. All it takes is one individual with an open heart to make a child feel safe, increase his self-worth, and help him find hope for his own future.

About the Author

William Anderson worked as an administrator in a faith-based children's agency in Missouri.

Danny

By William Anderson

"What a weary time those years were—to
have the desire and the need to live but not
the ability."

—Charles Bukowski, *Ham on Rye*

When Danny was eight, his mother left his father and him and cut off all contact with them. Danny's father, who was very passive, soon married a domineering woman. She wanted her new husband's undivided attention, and she started abusing Danny to make him so miserable that he would run away.

When he came home from school at 3 P.M., Danny would be sent to stand in a corner of the kitchen. For the next eight hours, he wasn't allowed to move. When Danny asked to use the bathroom, the stepmother said no. She would not let him sit down to do his homework. She would deny him dinner while she dined with his father in the next room. Danny's father was aware of the abuse of his son but did nothing.

Soaked in urine, Danny would raise a knee, which he used as a desk. When his leg became tired, he would switch to the other knee. His stepmother wouldn't let him sit on the floor. His father never intervened.

When children are bullied, abused, and intimidated, changes can occur in the area of the brain known as the amygdala, which is involved in the stress response. With a traumatized amygdala, children develop triggers that set off their fight or flight responses. They can overreact violently to nonthreatening actions by others. Striking out happens commonly, as do running away and self-harm.

Danny was too young and too frightened to fight back. He ran away several times. His stepmother punished him. Soon, Danny was forced to sleep in the basement with no bed, blankets, or bathroom. He slipped into a deep depression. During his basement exile, Danny mixed a jar of poisonous chemicals and set his eighteenth birthday for his suicide.

After more years of torture, Danny's stepmother put him in the custody of the state, which is defined as giving up parental rights to make decisions for one's child. His future was in the hands of Children's Division social workers.

The state sent Danny to foster homes, where older boys bullied him because he was afraid of everyone. Again, he ran away because he was too frightened to fight. Danny was sent to other foster homes, where he continued to be bullied. Danny self-harmed, ran away, and self-harmed more.

Occasionally Danny found solace and support in various churches along the way. "All I ever wanted was to be loved," he told every congregation that wanted to hear his story. Virtually every time Danny finished his talk, congregation members would hug him and tell him how strong he must be.

Danny was sent to multiple foster families and continued to run away. When he was fourteen, he was admitted to a privately-run children's home where Cindy, one of the therapists, took him under her wing. It was several months before Danny understood and accepted her affection. He had never been able to trust adults. Sometimes abused children can never trust again.

Danny had become hypervigilant. Common among children and adults who have repeatedly been treated badly, hypervigilance is a symptom of PTSD. With a damaged amygdala, these children are constantly monitoring their environments for threats. Danny wasn't able to sense Cindy's interest because he devoted all his attention to scanning for danger.

Danny had lost all hope that he could have a happy life with people who cared about him. He had planned to take his own life on his eighteenth birthday and had planned how he would do it. "I knew that when I turned eighteen, the state would emancipate me. So on my birthday, I would be sent out into the street with no high school diploma, no money, no job, and nowhere to live." That predicament is called "aging out."

Once Danny let Cindy in, she bonded with him personally, like a loving mother or aunt. She helped him raise his self-esteem, taught him new social skills, and gave him reasons he could have a good life.

Cindy insisted that the kids call her "Cindy Ma'am" because none of the children respected adults after years of abuse. Danny slipped and called her "Cindy Mama" one day and it stuck. With Cindy's guidance, Danny turned eighteen and did not commit suicide. Cindy made sure they celebrated.

Danny graduated from high school and enrolled in a state university. With Cindy's guidance, he bought a new car. A major health insurance company hired him, and he bought a house with Cindy's approval. Today Danny is forty, and he travels across the state speaking to audiences about the importance of resilience. And he still calls the woman who helped him Cindy Mama.

Medications can address depression and PTSD. Getting a child away from tormentors and into the care of a loving adult can help boys like Danny heal over time.

If you are being bullied, you can get help. There are people out there who know what you have been through. There are good people in the world. Go out and find them. Never give up.

About the Author

William Anderson worked as an administrator in a faith-based children's agency in Missouri.

You're Cool

By Adrian Preston

"Words can inspire. And words can destroy. Choose yours well."

– Robin Sharma, Author

"You're cool." I think those were the most important words anyone had ever said to me. I was twenty-three at the time, and I weighed 336 pounds.

I'd been a fat child who'd become a morbidly overweight adult. By age eleven, I weighed 154 pounds, and I gained 10 to 20 pounds a year until I topped the 336-pound mark.

You can imagine what the last dozen years of my life had been like. Every fat joke that had ever been thought of had been yelled in my face. Every fat gibe, too. To make matters worse, I bore an uncanny resemblance to a fat actor on a popular TV show, so everyone used to shout his character's name at me. Everyone—even people I didn't know.

Heck, I knew my position in life. I was worthless, a fat lump. Even my own father called me names—the one man in my life who should have been a rock for me. He made me feel worthless, too.

"You're cool."

The speaker of those words was a twelve-year-old boy. I used to play chess for a local club. So did he, and we were on the same team.

We lived close together, so for games where we played against other clubs, I used to drive him to the venues. We struck up a bond, and guess what . . . he liked me. He thought I was cool.

Really? After the dozens and dozens of people in my life who had abused me verbally, this one person—a kid, at that—actually liked me. He had the ability to see beyond the blubber and see the person beneath . . . and he thought that person was cool.

That's all it took. One person—twelve years old, under five feet tall, and less than a third of my body weight. If he could see the person beneath my fat body, why couldn't anyone else? Why couldn't I?

I decided I liked being thought of as "cool," so remembering those words, I dieted. I lost 154 pounds . . . in eleven months.

So, did everyone now think I was "cool"? Well, of course not, but people were a lot more willing to accept me as a decent guy rather than just someone to poke fun at in order to cheer themselves up. And yeah, some people *did* think I was cool.

I suddenly had a pool of really nice friends from whom stepped a lady I would go on to marry and father two children with. It started with a couple little words, someone believing in me, and me believing in myself.

While my personal experience was to undergo weight loss to get my health in order, I would not necessarily recommend drastic physical changes to everyone as the solution to their problems. What mattered most was that I found someone who believed in me and the motivation to show people who couldn't see past my exterior what a great person I was, and that I cared about myself.

I still think I'm cool. I have a pretty cool life—I'm forty-seven now with my own nicely flourishing business doing something I love. And lots of people whom I surround myself with think I'm cool, too. As for people who don't think I'm cool or begrudge me the happiness I've found . . . ah, screw 'em. . . .

If you're being bullied, like I was, then you're probably pretty cool, too, because being bullied makes you way cooler than all the bullies. You are much stronger and more resilient than they will ever know, but it can be hard to see how great you are. If you are used to being mistreated, you may take it for granted as if that's your situation in life. But it is not. All it takes is one person believing in you. And for you to believe in yourself.

And I am here to tell you that you are cool. Yeah, you're cool. You are wonderful and special. Just believe it yourself. Now, go out and do something about it.

About the Author

Adrian Preston is the pseudonym of a full-time freelance writer with his own successful copywriting business. He has had six books published, two e-books, over one hundred short stories, and five thousand articles. He still plays chess, albeit rather badly now.

How I Overcame Being Bullied

By Victoria Mask

"Do not pray for an easy life, pray for the
strength to endure a difficult one."
—Bruce Lee, Martial Artist

When I think of bullying, it does not seem that long ago that I felt alone. All through my public school experience, I was an outcast. My teachers and the people I considered friends stood by and watched while I was tormented. They did not intervene when perhaps they should have. Isolated, I became a target.

I first experienced bullying in elementary school. As a seven-year-old, I was teased because I was abandoned by my addict mother and raised by a single dad. I was an A and B student and never got in trouble. I turned my work in and certainly did not pick fights. I was bullied because I wasn't like everyone else. I didn't dress and act like the others—I had my own identity. The boys who were in my school would call me "Icky Vicky." The girls mocked me and made fun of my clothes. When I finally told my dad how they were treating me, he wrote a letter to my third-grade teacher to make her aware of the problem. The teacher proceeded to yell at me in front of my whole class! She claimed that I must have done something to provoke them. My third-grade teacher basically called me a liar. As you can imagine, my teacher's reaction made the situation worse.

The next year, horrible gossip was spread around the school by a popular girl. The girl acted as if she were my friend so she could come over to my house. She spent two nights and acted as though she'd had the most amazing time. On Monday morning, she told everyone that my dad poisoned the six-hour roast he cooked, that my house was a pig dive, and that we had no food, all of which was so made up, it was stupid. When I told people it wasn't true, the girl threatened to beat me up. Everyone looked at me as if I were a liar, and the people I looked to as friends turned against me. At such a young age, I felt no one wanted me.

For the next two years, mostly the same thing continued. I was befriended by the popular girls, who only wanted something in return. At first, I was treated like a true friend. They told me all their "secrets." The girls soon wanted me to give them the answers to homework, stack their chairs, and basically be their slave. In return, I got to be their "friend." One day I got so sick of it that I told one of the girls no. She got furious, so I was kicked out of their group. The girls then started to cyberbully me and spread lies about who they thought I was. They made the class not talk to me. I would go to school every day, and it was as if I were invisible, but they would still sling their insults my way.

In sixth grade, the boys would throw trash at me as if I were garbage. They acted as though I was their verbal punching bag. One boy would scream curse words at me from across the room. The girls would threaten me with fights. One boy and a girl actually slapped me! The teacher acted if she didn't hear or see what was going on. If I didn't ask the teachers to get involved, they would totally ignore the situation. When I did reach out for help, they always seemed to find a way to blame me.

And all of that was just in elementary school! When seventh grade started, I had high hopes. Most of my bullies were going to different schools. I thought I could start anew because most would not know about my past. I was only half right. School was good for the first month or two, but then it changed. There were two girls in my choir class who started out nice. They sat by me, and we would laugh about any little thing. But one day, out of the blue, they didn't sit by me or talk to me. I was a little confused and thought they were playing a joke because I did not want to believe that the bullying was starting again. When I went over to ask why they were ignoring me, one girl starting singing the whore song. It was so hurtful, and the girls around them started to sing it, too. They did not even turn their heads to see who they were singing the song to—they did it just to do it. It always made me speechless when someone called me a whore or slut because I've never even had a boyfriend. I felt so small and helpless. The two girls would proceed to get me in trouble in choir and drop me notes about how low of a person I was. They said I was a nobody and deserved to die. All I wanted was to fit in and be liked.

In eighth grade, my dad took me out of school. I have been homeschooled for two years now. I do believe, beyond a shadow of a doubt, that I would not be here if I were still in public school. I am a straight-A fifteen-year-old now, and I am going to college next year. It still brings me to tears remembering how I was treated. I am stronger, and I definitely know now that there is always something to live for. It is possible to come back from feeling worthless. You are worthy and even precious. There is always help, and someone will always care. I found that out before it was too late.

About the Author

Victoria Mask is a college-bound student. She has been homeschooled for the latter part of her high school career by her loving father. She looks forward to attending the school of her dreams in the coming year.

Stand Up Even If You Are Alone

By Sherri A.

"I always wondered why somebody didn't do
something about that; then I realized I am
somebody."

—Proverb, seen on Pinterest

When my son, Austin, was sixteen and my daughter, Alyssa, was fourteen, we had a very busy household. We live in a small town, and safety was never really a concern. We all knew our neighbors, and many of the kids had been together since they started grade school. When my kids asked one evening if they could go to Sonic for ice cream and then to Walmart for new headphones, it wasn't an issue. My husband and I told them to wear seat belts and not to stay out too late, as the next day was school.

Little did any of us know that our lives were about to be turned upside down. Two hours later, I got a frantic phone call from my son saying he was bleeding and on his way home. He was very upset. I barely recognized him when he walked into the house. Imagine our horror when we saw him with blood all down his face and an eye practically swollen shut. His nose was to the side and obviously broken. We immediately took him to the emergency room.

After four hours, we were sent home. The injuries included a broken nose, twelve stitches above the eye, facial lacerations, and a fractured ankle. He also had a black eye and the other eye almost swollen shut. While we were at the ER, the police were called and they were very helpful. After talking with my son and my daughter, and based on the injuries, they had enough evidence to make an arrest.

A young man in my son's school had set him up at the Walmart parking lot. Through mutual friends, he knew where my son was going to be. The video at Walmart showed my two kids and four other kids walking out of Walmart. Unfortunately, my kids parked by a light in the parking lot. All that was recorded there was a very bright light.

The kid who assaulted my son came from around the side of the pickup and threw him down. Then he used his knee to damage Austin's face and then stomped on him. Then all the kids involved got into their vehicle and drove away. These were all kids we knew, and four of the five had been to my house on several occasions.

The young man who assaulted my son was upset because Austin talked to his girlfriend—a girl he had known for many years and had been friends with for a long time. The perpetrator had also assaulted two other kids earlier (we didn't know this until their parents came forward later). He assumed that we would ignore it, as they did. That's where he was wrong.

My kids absolutely amazed me through it all. Austin had to have nose surgery and was on crutches for two months. It was winter, and it was icy outside. He missed a great deal of school due to his injuries and medical appointments. We also had concerns at school because the boys had classes together. With only twenty-five kids in the junior class, you can imagine what it was like.

We went to the school the day after it happened with a restraining order, and they blew us off. They said until he was convicted of a crime, there wasn't much they could do. We weren't about to allow that to continue. We went to the school board, and they at least established some guidelines for keeping the boys separated.

This young man and his family were angry that we pressed charges. He was a good athlete, and they were worried about how a police record would affect him. They never apologized or asked how my son was doing. They never thought about my daughter, who had witnessed the violence.

My family struggled because suddenly our town was divided. Some had heard that it was boys being boys and Austin had lost a fight, so they didn't think it was right to press criminal charges. There was also an outpouring of support from friends, family, and people we didn't know to help get the issue resolved.

After sentencing, we went back to the school and were told that we should focus on forgiveness. It didn't help our case that the superintendent is best friends with the mother of the boy who assaulted Austin, and his dad is a sports coach at the school.

At that point, we went to the media and Facebook. Within hours of posting pictures and information about the situation, we had thousands of comments and newfound support. The local news channel contacted us and ran the story. The fact that the perpetrator is an out-of-district student who was allowed to stay didn't sit well.

Upon getting the community and media involved, the school was under fire. They had no choice but to deliver a solid plan of action to help us. This included ensuring that the boys wouldn't be in the same class together. As seniors by the time of sentencing, there were classes such as government that only one teacher offered. Austin has been able to take them through the local college and get credit for them.

I am in awe of my kids and how they handled the situation. I wanted them both to go to different schools after this occurred. They wouldn't consider it. Austin said he didn't do anything wrong, and he wasn't going to be run off from the school he wanted to attend.

So many kids have come forward since that day to talk about bullying in our school—many parents, too. It appears that it has been an ongoing issue for quite some time, and the school administration and school board just ignore it. They can't do that anymore because people are no longer looking the other way.

Austin once told me that if it hadn't happened to him, the perpetrator would have assaulted more kids. It had to stop, and we were the ones who had to stand up and fight for changes. Our family has been on a long journey to healing. It is still hard to let the kids go out and be teenagers because we know what can happen.

However, I am very proud of how they have helped start conversations about bullying at school and drive home the fact that by standing up for what is right, we can all make a difference. That experience is the positive outcome of what occurred. We all have the power to stand up for what is right. It isn't always easy, but it can make a difference and it has to be done.

About the Author

Sherri is forty-two years old and works from home as a freelance writer. She lives with her husband, a truck driver, and three children, ages twenty, eighteen, and fourteen. She and her family live in a small town in Colorado.

Part VI: Perseverance

"The brick walls are there for a reason. The brick walls are not there to keep us out. The brick walls are there to give us a chance to show how badly we want something. Because the brick walls are there to stop the people who don't want it badly enough. They're there to stop the other people."

--Randy Pausch, Lecturer

Small-Town Kid

By James Clark

"If you are going through hell, keep going."
—Winston Churchill

As a kid, I went to a small school—a really small school. There were about 150 of us spread over nine years, which meant that we would often attend mixed-year classes. That made it pretty easy to be one of the cool kids, and between my being fairly tall and having fashionably spiky hair, I was well liked by the girls and respected by the boys. All in all, life was pretty good.

All of that changed soon after I turned fourteen—an awkward age for any kid—when my dad was offered a new job and we moved several hours away. Because I had grown up in a tiny community where everyone knew everyone else, I had never known that I was shy and socially awkward around new people. How could I? Everyone I had reason to talk to I had known more or less since I was born.

Five minutes after walking into my new school, I pretty much figured out that I suffered from crippling social anxiety around new people. I had no idea what to say or how to make new friends, and no clue how to deal with being shunned by my peers.

These were city kids—really cool kids of the type I had only ever seen on TV and assumed were entirely fictional, like any other villainous character that tortured average nice folk like myself.

Halfway through my first day, I was informed that my accent was unacceptable because apparently I sounded like an old-timey farmer, and it was impossible to understand what I said, let alone take me seriously. To top it off, my clothes were painfully uncool; baggy jeans were all the rage in the country, so that's all I had, but in my new school I might as well have been wearing a diaper.

As if that wasn't enough, I would soon find out that the level of education at my old school could only be described as thoroughly subpar. Most of the time I had no clue what was going on in class, and it didn't take long for my classmates to figure that one out, either. All of a sudden, I had gone from being smart and cool—the kid most likely to succeed both in life and with the ladies—to being the most incomprehensibly uncool loser you could imagine. I probably don't need to tell you that there was no shortage of kids to point that out to me, either.

A month or so after arriving at my new school, I walked past a couple—a boy and a girl—unashamedly sharing a seat and kissing in the common area. They were in my grade and were considered pretty cool. As I hurriedly shuffled past, pretending I had somewhere to go when in reality I was on my way to the bathroom to spend the remaining thirty minutes of my lunch break, they asked me to sit down in the armchair across from theirs. They were nice, asked me where I was from, and tried to get to know me. The relief of someone actually being nice lasted for about five minutes. An older boy walked up and told me to move, and when I refused, he promptly threw his considerably heftier body atop mine and proceeded as though I wasn't there. There was nothing I could do but sit there, humiliated, until finally he went to class.

Not long after that, I was walking down a corridor on my own. Uncharacteristically, I had a smile on my face, and naturally another older boy caught me expressing this (for me) forbidden emotion. As he walked past, he shoved me into the wall and asked me, "What the [h-word] are you smiling for? [F-word] loser." Life would pretty much continue along those lines for another few months until I was accepted by a ragtag gang of "nerds." Having been a "cool" kid in my previous school, I essentially had nothing in common with these kids—I wasn't half as smart as they were, hadn't studied anywhere near as hard, and didn't share any of their interests. Still, they took me in, and before long I was left alone by the meaner kids and was safe in the midst of the new group. Slowly but surely, I came out of my shell. I became happier because I had people to talk to, and I started taking school more seriously than I ever had before.

Despite my newfound motivation to study, I was far behind from the offset and never managed to catch up. When the time came to move on to high school, my grades weren't good enough to get into the same classes as my friends, who all studied natural science. Instead, I ended up taking classes with kids who weren't quite as cool, but nearly, and most of them were from rough backgrounds (which mine was not—I come from a very loving middle-class family). This made my social anxiety far worse. It got to the point where I was so scared of being made fun of that I couldn't be the first to leave a classroom for fear of not being able to open the door—which would make me look like an idiot. I couldn't talk to people I didn't know. I couldn't press the stop button on the bus without sweating, hyperventilating, and nearly fainting from anxiety because I was scared that the button wouldn't work and I would have to stand up— in front of everyone—to reach another button.

What did remain was my motivation to study harder, which I did. A year or so into high school, I made a friend, then two, then three. They wanted to get better grades, so they asked to study with me. In return, they helped me come out of my shell and showed me that people weren't out to hurt me or laugh at me. I can't overstate how grateful I am for that, and I'm friends with one of them to this day despite the fact that I moved abroad nearly a decade ago.

After high school, I moved abroad to be with a girl I had met through an online game. She was going to college, so I applied, too. The move, and going to college, meant going further outside my comfort zone than I would have ever thought possible—but it's the best thing I have ever done. I ended up graduating at the top of my class, winning five awards for academic excellence, and being accepted into a PhD program. For that, I thank my bunch of "nerdy" friends. I talked to people and made more, and better, friends than I could ever have dreamed of. Now I even stand up in front of two hundred students and deliver lectures! For that, I thank the "rough" kids at my high school. Finally, I found love. For that, I'm just thankful.

If you had told the kid who didn't dare smile in school, who couldn't open a door or press a stop button, that this was how his life would work out, he wouldn't have believed you. Some days, he still doesn't.

Being bullied is an unfortunate circumstance of some people just being jerks. But if you are suffering now, it doesn't mean you always will. People can be awful, but there are good people out there. Sometimes it just takes work to find them. Keep trying and one day you'll find that you succeed.

I'm not sure what advice I would give to someone who is being bullied. I think it really depends on the situation, and in a lot of instances the best thing to do is to gather the courage to talk to someone—a parent, guidance counselor, teacher, or anyone you can trust. When you're in the midst of a bad situation, it's often hard to see a way out, even though it may be right in front of you.

For kids who are going through something similar to what I went through, I think it's important to work on having the confidence to be yourself. Being bullied, or even just a bit of a social outcast, can make your forget that you have just as much right to exist and be true to yourself as anyone else. That's easier said than done, but I'm a living testament to the fact that it can be done—and it's worth all the hard work.

About the Author

James Clark is the pseudonym of a freelance writer from a small town in the United Kingdom. He has over five years of experience as a content creator and marketer. Graduating in the top of his class, he is now pursuing a doctorate in consumer research.

From Victim to Victor

By Thirumur David Kiran

"The only way out of the labyrinth of
suffering is to forgive."
—John Green, Author

As any teenager will attest, figuring out your identity in adolescence is real struggle. Forget the fact that you're experiencing hormonal changes, too. You are just one kid in a world of plenty. You're one of X number of siblings (nine, in my case), in a neighborhood of a hundred, in a school of a thousand, in a city of six million, in a country of one billion, in a world of seven billion and growing. You're a small fish in a gigantic ocean. "Insignificant," you may tell yourself. And so you go about trying to establish your identity and carve out your little place on the planet—a way that people can see you and know who you are. Some take up sports; others take up fashion. Some develop their looks; others develop their minds. Others get tattoos or bikes or fancy cars. And others get tough and try to exert their "authority" on those poor less fortunate souls around them. Believe me, I know. I was one of those "unfortunate souls" who fell victim to the sea of kids trying to figure themselves out.

Being a teenager is only a small portion of our existence, and we often look back on our youth when we are older and laugh at our stupidity. Yet while we are young, everything seems like such an ordeal. Our bodies are growing, and every day we're experiencing new things that we have no clue about. We suddenly find ourselves with a changing body, facial hair, pimples, and a load of testosterone. We begin to notice the opposite sex more and feel the need to impress and socialize—no matter how awkwardly. And everything becomes categorized and compartmentalized. School = Boring. Parties = Fun. Intelligent Person = Nerd. Socialite = Popular. Athletes = Cool. NEBs (Non-Energetic Bodies—a term used in our peer group to describe people who didn't have an athletic bone in their body) = not so much. And then we mentally assign tasks to those categories. School = Do as little as possible. Parties = Attend as many as you can. Intelligent Person = Mingle with only when tests are coming up. Socialite = Mingle with whenever possible. Athletes = Adore and idolize. NEBs = Avoid like the plague.

I fell into the category of a NEB. Like NEBs and nerds, I was part of the lowest tier in the pecking order. Together, we formed the "un-cool" club. This meant a lot of things.

"Un-cool" because we weren't as good-looking as the others.

"Un-cool" because we weren't as strong or athletic as the others.

"Un-cool" because we were shy and a wee bit introverted.

Or, generally "un-cool" because we weren't like the rest of "them."

Now, the "un-cool" club wasn't really a club per se. It was more of a lack of one. An evolution of sorts. It was like a group of kids with no money looking through the window of an ice cream store at all the other kids inside with their ice cream cones, wishing for just one bite. And so we'd look at all the Socialites, the Athletes, and the other cool folks having a great and wonderful time (or, at least, we thought they were—you know, the "grass is greener on the other side" adage and all), and we really wished we could get into that group. Yet we couldn't.

Oddly enough, after a little while, the "cool" club would run out of things to do. They would then decide to pick on the "un-cool" kids to boost their own feelings of "coolness." This was how the bullying culture in my peer group started.

As one of the social outcasts, I was bullied a lot by my peers in a variety of ways.

For starters, I was excluded from parties, even ones you'd think I would be invited to just because it would be polite. I remember being locked out from a party that was organized in my own dorm room. I spent the night in my brother's bunk.

I was the last one to be picked for any kind of activity. Sometimes I wasn't even picked at all. There's nothing more agonizing than standing in the middle of a room when teams are being assembled and everyone is getting selected but you. You get your hopes up every time the designated captains open their mouths to call a name, only to be dashed when another name is called instead. I'll never forget the time when teams were being selected for a game of soccer. I was actually a pretty decent goalie and had quick reflexes. There were two people left to be chosen. Me and Tommy. Tommy had a broken leg. Tommy got chosen.

I could never find a partner for a dance. This was not for lack of trying. Every girl that I approached spurned me—not all of them nicely, either. There was one girl I really loved (as teenagers love). I did everything I could to win her over. I held the door open for her, cleaned her desk, carried her bags, sneaked chocolate into her dresser, and even did her homework assignments—until I finally had the courage to ask her out. Her response? "Get out of my way, fatty!"

Unfortunately, I was laughed at and called names. "Fatty" was one of the more charitable ones. Once I was cornered in the locker room after a swim in the pool and was tossed out without any clothes. Worse than the sheer embarrassment of being naked was the fact that I got put on detention for it. In defense of my teachers, they didn't see the events leading up to me streaking through the hallway—only the actual streaking. A school no-no for sure!

I was also physically abused. There was a big guy in our group called Phil. He would take out his testosterone mood swings on me. If anything in his day went wrong, I was the one singled out for it. And by singled out, I mean cornered and punched repeatedly. Missed the ball in sports? My fault. Scored low on a test? My fault. Girlfriend didn't talk to him that day? My fault. Detention? My fault. And there was nothing I could do about it. The one time I tried fighting back, he got a bunch of his buddies to find me later that evening.

I could never explain the bruises to my parents. I was too afraid to. Would they understand? Would they report it to the principal? If they did, what would happen next? I was sure I'd be labeled a "tattletale" swiftly thereafter. And surely the lecture Phil would receive would cause him to have a bad day and for this whole cycle to repeat. No, it was better to say nothing and cite the usual excuses of a "playground accident" or "sporting injury" rather than to invite more abuse—or so I thought.

Those weren't the worst things that happened to me, though. The hardest thing about being bullied and excluded from social activities is the emotional pain that goes with it. You can put up with the physical pain, but the emotional stuff destroys you. You begin to question your own worth, your place, your very existence. You wonder why you are alive at all and if what everyone says about you is actually true.

I know I am not alone in this. There were many other "un-cool" folks like me who suffered similar or worse fates. But the oddest thing—and to this day, I can't figure out why—is that instead of forming our own social group and being happy with ourselves and our designated "un-coolness," we each sought to get ourselves into the "cool" club and to appear "cool" like they were. We avoided the other "outcasts" of the group, thinking that perhaps if we avoided the other "un-cool" kids, we'd magically evolve into "cool" characters. But it never worked. We remained outcasts. Lonely outcasts.

The breaking point for me happened one year when summer camp coincided with my birthday. I attended a coed camp, so there were a lot more emotions present. I had kept the fact that it was my birthday a secret (not that the others attendees cared to know anyway), but my sister, who was attending the same camp, spilled the beans to one of the counselors, who planned a surprise after the evening activity.

The evening came and went, and the activity was complete when one of the counselors burst out of the kitchen with a cake and began singing "Happy Birthday." The other counselors joined in while the campers looked around the room, confused. But as soon as my name was mentioned, something happened that shattered my fourteen-year-old world—the room emptied. Almost without exception, the campers began to stream out. I was shattered, and I also headed out as fast as I could. I found a quiet place, hid there, and cried my eyes out for hours. I had never felt so alone or forsaken as I did at that moment. The thought of taking my life occurred to me, yet by the grace of God I had the strength to suck it up and return to camp.

But amazingly, my breaking point was also my turning point. A nearly identical scenario followed a few days later with another camper—a nerd. A similar exodus occurred. But I stayed. I sang along and shared wishes and bought her a gift. She later became my best friend. Lo and behold, she transformed and eventually became the most popular person in the school. Yet we remained close friends. We even dated for a while.

As my teen years progressed, I grew out of my NEB stage. I got taller and stronger. I took up sports. I became popular. I got my first job at fifteen and made more money than the rest of my peers. And I slowly gained their respect. A number of them even became my close friends. Bullying has a time and then it passes. People change. The ones who are on the receiving end become tougher for it; many of the ones who administer it grow out of it and then feel terrible for what they did. It's essential to let go of the past. Time not only heals all wounds, it also puts things into perspective. One of my first employees when I founded my first company (a social entrepreneurship start-up) was Phil, the guy who used to punch me.

I credit a lot of my change to a few close friends, an incredible teacher who was a mentor for me, my faith in God, and my decision to make something of my life. Up until that point, I was so wrapped up in trying to make a good impression on others that I wasn't focused on creating a life for myself. But nothing I did to impress others worked. My mentor helped me realize that my life was my own and that I had the choice to determine what I wanted out of life and then to go out and get it.

Today I am a happy and successful person with no permanent damage from the bullying I received. It's not that the wounds weren't there. It's just that they have been healed and the scars have faded. However, it wasn't the success that healed my heart. It was the forgiving. I lived through some painful years, but I believe that you can either live as a prisoner of your past or you can make something of your future. I chose to accept, forgive, and move on. As such, I have been healed, and all that remains are the things I learned from the experience—empathy, sympathy, understanding, care, maturity, love, and how to have a tough skin. These traits enable me not only to be successful in business but also to help others. Who better to help those going through a rough time than those who have been through it themselves?

My hope and prayer for you, dear reader, is that if you are being bullied, you won't give up hope! Things will change. This phase will pass. It might seem like the end of the world, but it doesn't have to be. And you're not alone. Reach out to those around you who are suffering the same fate. They'll become some of your closest friends. And if you are someone who is bullying others—either intentionally or unintentionally—I implore you to consider your actions and change them. Put yourself in their shoes because maybe you will be there one of these days. There are other ways to have an identity without attempting to put others down. You can be popular, successful, happy, and cool—AND be kind and caring. In fact, those attributes will make you even more so.

May God help us to have a world of kindness and love.

About the Author

Thirumur David Kiran is a social entrepreneur, speaker, and youth training professional who works across India and the United States. In his own words, "I am passionate about people and about making a difference in their lives. I believe that every human being is designed for greatness, and my passion is to help each person discover that greatness and grow into it."

Never Give Up

By Kannan Karthik M.

"Never give up on something you really want.
It's difficult to wait, but it's worse to regret."
—Unknown

Vijayan came from a very humble family. Both of his parents were daily wage laborers who worked for construction sites. They always had difficulty making ends meet. Although poor, Vijayan's parents put their son first and insisted that he attend school. Vijayan loved school. Though he was not academically bright, he loved to understand things from a practical perspective. Every one of his relatives objected to him attending school. They were of the opinion that he, too, should be a laborer and should earn money to help support the household, as is typical in India. Vijayan's situation was perhaps not helped by the fact that, although eager to attend school, he was not considered a very bright pupil.

Things turned against him when he failed to pass the tenth grade board exams, which are required in order to enter college in India. Vijayan was not only poor and born to a backward caste, but now he had also failed, according to everyone's expectations. This opened the door for all sorts of bullying and sarcasm. Every relative came forward with, "Look, I was right" admonishments—perhaps the cruelest form of bullying, as one might expect at least family members to be supportive. For a fourteen-year-old, this was a bit too much to take. So Vijayan put his educational dreams on hold.

He had no choice but to work as a child laborer to earn a living. There were no social security programs in India at the time. His family *was* poor and they *did* need money. Child labor is banned in India, but the practice is widespread. Blue-collar laborers are highly exploited in India, and they receive very little respect and remuneration for their work. As a minor, Vijayan was subjected to a great deal of exploitation at his workplace and was often bullied and overworked without fair compensation. It may not be wrong to say that he earned peanuts for the work he did. Being short, timid, and darker skinned than most others all worked against him. His coworkers and supervisors used these as excuses to single him out. In his later years, he'd recount how this kind of treatment made him stronger, both mentally and physically.

Despite the poor treatment, he kept his dreams alive in his heart. He was practical enough to accept his current situation and keep working, ignoring the bullying and the negative environment around him. He continued to work as a cement mixer for the next five years, until he was nineteen years old. The working conditions were substandard, and he was often roughed up and humiliated through no fault of his own. This is a common technique used in Indian factories to break down laborers and make them work as slaves.

In India, you earn the right to vote when you turn eighteen. Election ID cards are then distributed. When Vijayan turned nineteen, he was able to apply for his tenth grade board exam—an exam most students pass at age fourteen. He submitted his election

ID card as proof of residence.

At the department of examinations, his application made waves. Comments ranged from "Why is this uncle appearing for the exam?" to "He is destined to be a cement mixer, so why should he waste his life passing an exam?" and "He is good for nothing." Every pessimist crawled out from every corner to try to "convince" him not to waste his time taking this exam. People took every opportunity to knock him down. But Vijayan remained resolute.

When the exam results were announced a few months later, he had managed to pass—just barely. The bullying, instead of dwindling, increased. When he returned to work, he was greeted with, "Here comes our overqualified cement mixer." On top of it all, his workload increased with next to no increase in pay. So he decided to make a move.

After passing the tenth grade exam, Vijayan applied for a job in a soap-making factory. This was a slightly better job, as it meant he could save for college. As expected, his college plan was not something his relatives approved of. They were of the opinion that he should give all the extra money to the family and not be selfish. He did send a portion of the money home so as to make sure all of his family was fed, but he kept the remainder for the pursuit of his dream.

Things took a bad turn when there was a suspected robbery in the factory and all the blue-collar laborers were rounded up by police officers. They were taken to the police station for interrogation. Indian interrogations are unlike anything that happens in the West.

All kinds of human rights violations take place during the course of an interrogation, including suspects being beaten and stripped in most cases. Electrocutions even take place in some extreme cases. In this robbery case, too, the laborers were mistreated. These are the most vulnerable people in society who have nobody to vouch for them. Police officers usually take advantage of them for that reason.

They were all later acquitted due to lack of evidence, but the stigma of being picked up for a robbery remained with Vijayan. The bullying and criticism continued, but with much greater impact. He was fired from his job and was unable to find another one due to the stigma of being a robbery suspect.

It is said that adverse situations can either make or break a person. That was certainly true for Vijayan. Fortunately, he had saved enough for his college tuition and was able to enroll in a program to earn a bachelor's degree in economics. There were quite a few young kids in his neighborhood, and he started tutoring them in the evening to earn a living. This routine continued for the next few years, with the number of students he tutored growing in number. Vijayan soon became "Vijayan Sir" who taught economics to high school kids.

His rather simplified way of teaching attracted a large number of students to his evening tutoring center. In the meantime, five more years passed, and by this time Vijayan was a mature adult in his mid-twenties. With his savings, he was able to obtain a master's degree in economics. Even with this reasonable improvement in his situation, his dreams did not stop there.

Next, Vijayan started to prepare for the prestigious Indian civil services exam, and the bullying and taunting came back to haunt him.

People said things like, "You are not cut out for it," "You are dark," "You are not brilliant," and, worst of all, "You were thrown out of a soap factory, and now you are competing for the top jobs." He had heard and seen all these things for far too long.

(A note on Indian civil services: This is the entry pass to the top jobs in government, whether administration, police, customs, forestry, or engineering services. Many candidates take the exam, but only a few hundred pass.)

In 1999, Vijayan submitted an application to work at the Sardar Vallabhai National Police Academy in Hyderabad, India. He submitted his application to an attendant who verified Vijayan's academic records and noticed his late passing of tenth grade. But the reaction was different this time. "That's some remarkable progress, Sir." For someone who was thrown out of a soap factory and denied menial jobs because he was picked up by the police, it was a remarkable achievement to join the top police academy in the country to train as a senior officer.

Vijayan passed in 2000. He opted to serve his home cadre in Kerala and joined as Assistant Commissioner of Police in the state capital. Over the years since 2000, he was instrumental in solving many cold trail investigations. But his most prestigious achievement was the social reforms he undertook.

Many petty crimes were taking place in slum neighborhoods on the outskirts of Trivandrum, and coming from a humble background, Vijayan knew exactly the reason and cure for the situation. Young people get bullied and ridiculed there, and they turn to crime for easy money. His cure was simple—give them respect with responsibility.

Many young slum boys who had just turned eighteen were recruited as temporary traffic wardens in the city. The uniform gave them respect among their peers. The satisfaction of experiencing all the big, swanky German- and American-built cars stopping at the signal of their hand cannot be expressed in words. True to Vijayan's expectation, the crime rate dropped.

I last met Vijayan when he was transferred out of the state capital and given the greater responsibility of handling the intelligence bureau. Though he never considers himself a role model, he is for many people. This year he was nominated as the "CNN-IBN Indian of the Year"—a prestigious award given to exceptional people by the CNN-IBN news channel. The awards are given for different fields, including public administration, health care, and humanitarian work. His nomination was a testament to his many contributions.

With the odds stacked against him, Vijayan made his seemingly impossible dreams come true. Many people did not believe in him, but he believed in himself. Through perseverance, Vijayan was able to accomplish goal after goal. The son of cement laborers was able to graduate from tenth grade, then college, and then graduate school. He became a civil servant and intelligence bureau officer. He impacted not only his life but also the lives of many others. He went from being someone who was disrespected by his own family, to eventually being lauded by an entire country.

About the Author

Kannan Karthik M. is a native of Trivandrum, India, and is a software engineer by profession. After serving for over three years with a software company in Trivandrum, he was admitted to an MBA program at Amity University, New Delhi. He completed his MBA with majors in IT and marketing. Presently, he is serving as an assistant manager in WellCare Infotech, Dubai, UAE.

Survival Mode

By Anonymous

""We could do it, you know."

"What?"

"Leave the district. Run off. Live in the

woods.

You and I, we could make it.""

—Suzanne Collins, *The Hunger Games*

You can be bullied by anyone. In my case, it was my parents. On the outside, we were a pretty normal family. At least that's what my dad said when he hit me or called me stupid. He'd say, "At least we can pass as respectable to outsiders." Between bruisings, I found that small consolation.

My mom would tell me that I deserved to get hit because I was bad, as in a bad person. But I think she just said that because she was in denial that there was an issue—and it wasn't my fault. When my dad punched a hole in the wall with his fists while trying to break into a bathroom where she had locked herself after an argument they had while she was pregnant, I don't think she believed she was bad and deserved to hide. As humans are prone to, she simply chose to ease her conscience by believing that there was something wrong with her child rather than have to confront the larger issue that there might be something wrong with the treatment of her child.

As a child, I knew from watching TV shows like *Full House* that being slapped on the arms until you bruise was not normal—especially not when your parents try to make you wear long sleeves to hide it. Or when they try to shame you into not telling others. When they tell your grandparents they only ever spanked you, when in actuality you were slapped, pinched, pushed, and shoved on a regular basis. When they threaten to hit, kill, or sell you almost every day. When they yell at you whenever they had a bad day at work. When they use fists instead of words to express themselves to someone half their size.

Growing up was rough for me because my friends had normal, loving parents. I didn't think they would have been able to relate to me or understand, so I hid it. They thought my parents were normal because they let me go on field trips and paid for my activity fees. In public, my parents were involved and concerned about my well-being. They would show up for parent-teacher conferences. They would ask how I was doing. To the public, this showed that they "cared." Oddly enough, we did pass on the exterior as a regular family. We lived in an affluent suburb. My parents both had white-collar jobs. I attended public school. I got good grades—even straight As. I made friends. I was active in many clubs and sports. However, there was something very different about us beneath the surface.

My friends did not know the truth. They didn't understand why I wore rags to school every day even though I lived in a nice house in a rich part of town. They thought I chose to dress that way—in hand-me-downs and clothes with holes. For a long time, the only clothes I got were on my birthday from visiting relatives or my parents' friends' children's used garments. I wasn't "good" so I didn't deserve proper clothes. I didn't earn "income" so I contributed nothing. On a regular basis, my parents told me that I wasted their money. They made me feel bad for spending their hard-earned cash on food, shelter, existence. . . . In hindsight, there was nothing I could do to repay them for the "debt of life" I was so generously given. I would try to do chores, but they would tell me that I did them wrong and just made more work for them to have to clean up. When I got sick, they would tell me that it was my fault because I didn't wear enough clothes and that I wasted their time because I forced them to take care of me. As a result, TV became my escape. I would watch shows and see how others lived. . . . But from that, at least, I grew to understand that my life was not normal.

My parents were a contradiction. They told me that I needed to study hard. They would pay for my college education. But they also told me I was dumb and would be lucky if I got into college. Their proof was when I finally got bad grades. Even then, they didn't seem to understand cause and effect. I had trouble paying attention in school because I got no sleep as a result of recurring nightmares. My grades plummeted from top of the class to bottom. I was worried all the time. When I went to school, I would worry about my grades. When I got home, I would worry about whether my parents were in a good mood. Being young in a bad home was stressful. They would hit me and then tell me that they only did it because they loved me. They would excuse behaviors that I knew did not represent love.

Often I would sit down to study but find myself having trouble focusing. Simple math problems became difficult. Word problems were confusing. My vision quickly deteriorated. When I would try to write out problems, my dad would tell me my handwriting was hideous. I would tear out a page to start over, and he would slap me because he said that showed attitude. When I cried, he would start hitting me as if consumed by guilt or fervor. My little brother would ask my mom why my dad was hitting me. She would shush him out of the room and say that it was because I was being bad. My father later said, by way of explanation, that I had made my notebook asymmetrical; I had wasted paper and thus deserved to be punished. The sheer lack of reason and insanity were disturbing. Living with my parents was like living with a ticking bomb that continuously reset.

Nonetheless, my relatives didn't have a clue as to what was going on. When I slept over at my cousin's house as a child, my uncle and aunt teased me in the morning. They asked if I always cried in my sleep. They thought it was cute. What could possibly make an eight-year-old cry at night? I didn't sleep the next night until after they had fallen asleep so I was sure they wouldn't hear me cry.

Even decades later, I still vividly remember everything that happened. Being treated horrifically left a mark on me. I am not a totally healed person. The scars I carry will probably always be there since they were a large part of my development, but I consider myself successful because I was able to escape from my parents' influence and have been able to thrive despite adversity. I learned how to avoid or cope with negative influences and how to surround myself with positive energy. Despite the fact that my own family told me I was stupid and a waste of money, I was able to successfully graduate from college and am on my way to completing graduate school, which I am paying for. I was able to get a great job in the field I am interested in—helping other people. I was able to find a slice of personal happiness and create a home for myself. I was able to do these things because I believe that I am fundamentally a good and worthy person. I am not stupid. Nor am I bad. I never believed that—no matter what they said.

Later on in life, I learned that my father had been severely beaten as a child by his mother. She had experienced significant mental problems throughout her life. Her friends and family had tried to get her on medication as an adult, but it is unclear whether she ever got proper treatment. Strangers and acquaintances had gone as far as calling her evil. I don't think she was evil. I think she may have also been abused. The cycle perpetuated itself. But I know it will stop with me because I recognize it for what it is. It is wrong.

Other people's mental problems should not become your problems. Their burden is not your burden. If you have experienced similar hardship, you are not alone. Go out and explore the world. Experience the good and surround yourself with it. The planet is a much bigger place—filled with wonder and amazement—than those with small minds would have you think. If you are not appreciated somewhere, find the place where you belong.

It is difficult if you are being bullied by someone who should be supporting you. But not everyone in the world is warped. There are good, kind, gentle forces in the world as well. Seek them out. Never, ever let someone tell you that you are anything less than what you want to be.

About the Author

Anonymous is a freelancer. Besides seeing the world from a TV screen when she was growing up, she has since been able to travel it. Her hobbies include meeting new people and learning about new cultures.

Part VII: Yourself

"Never grow a wishbone where your
backbone ought to be."
—Clementine Paddleford, Journalist

The Swan

By Laura P

"Beauty is not in the face; beauty is a light in
the heart."

— Kahlil Gibran, Artist and Poet

As a young girl with glasses, bad skin, and a height that outpaced nearly all of her male and female peers in middle school, I was a prime target for bullying. Even though I had a good group of friends, I was shocked when I received a forwarded email from another friend who had been looped in on a chain message discussing my "ratty hair."

The bullying got worse when my pants were pulled down in front of the entire orchestra as it was preparing to practice. I became convinced there was something wrong with me that was inviting this kind of behavior, but I tried my best to avoid responding to it. This kind of treatment, frequently aimed at making me feel like I was an "odd duck," persisted for years.

It was not easy to get through, but I chose to instead focus on growing as a person and spending time with people who did not bully others. Removing myself from any situation where bullying was present and reporting incidents of bullying to adults kept me from being involved any further.

Whether you want it to or not, nasty comments and bullying behavior do affect you. It's very hard, if not impossible, to let bullying behavior just roll off your back. Where you do have control, however, is in how you respond to it. Initially, the comments and behavior were extremely hurtful to me, but I decided that the best approach was to try and better myself and stay out of the fray. I removed myself from social situations where I felt the bullying could happen and instead focused on my most positive relationships with my friends.

Surrounding myself with positive people who shared the same interests certainly didn't stop the bullying, but it did reinforce that not everyone found that behavior to be appropriate. Being surrounded by people striving to reach their dreams regardless of what others thought fueled me forward and encouraged me to believe I could be whatever I want to be, even if a select group of people at school didn't think I was "cool" enough. These people who focused on bullying spent so much time being negative that they missed out not only on getting to know me but also on spending more time improving their own lives.

The mentality that I should pursue my aspirations and network with other people who also believed in that has carried me a long way. Since graduating from high school, I've been a Miss Virginia semifinalist, received more than $80,000 in scholarships for college and graduate school, been awarded three university-wide commendations for my community service related to mentoring, lived abroad in England, and began my PhD degree. I currently own a six-figure freelance writing and coaching business from the comfort of my own home. What I have learned from this is that dedicating yourself to becoming all you aspire to and not allowing others to tear you down can lead you on a very powerful path. Throughout your life, there will always be people who laugh at you or tell you that you can't do it. If you believe what they say, these bullies will be right. It may be one of the hardest things you'll ever have to do, but you should always avoid these people or reply politely but curtly. Don't waste your energy on these people. Instead, seek out the support network of the people who believe in your abilities and who push you to accomplish incredible things.

Bullying is not easy for anyone to put up with. Deciding how much energy you're going to let it drain from you, however, is your choice. Choose instead to spend your time with people who care about you—both friends and family. Being around positive individuals can go a long way toward supporting you in achieving your biggest dreams.

About the Author

Obtaining her goals, Laura P. is a PhD candidate at Virginia Tech as well as a small business owner. She wants to motivate young people to have the courage to follow their passions, as following hers has led her to happiness.

Like Oil and Vinegar

By Rosemary K.

"You yourself, as much as anybody in the
entire universe, deserve your love and
affection"
—Gautama Buddha, Spiritual Leader

They say, "birds of a feather flock together." And they also say, "opposites attract." It was more a case of the latter when I met Jeff. In some ways we were pretty similar, but mostly we were complete opposites. Not only were our personalities very different, but we were also from very different cultural backgrounds.

Being an avid bird lover, if I were to compare Jeff and me to our counterparts in the world of birds, I would see him as an eagle and myself as a dove. He was the confident one, the natural leader, the one who always knew what to do, who liked to fly high and catch the currents of the wind. I was a homely bird who liked to sit in my nest or sing peacefully in the trees, taking care of my young.

I saw our opposite qualities as an asset and thought we could complement each other: whatever he lacked I could make up for, and vice versa. However, he would use these differences to tell me that I was wrong, and he would often ask in an exasperated tone, "What is wrong with you?" I soon got the message that his way was the only right way. The sad part was that deep down inside, I agreed with him and thought that there really must be something horribly wrong with me. He was obviously such a confident and seemingly successful person, so he must be right and therefore I must be wrong. I discovered that the eagle whose strong wings I had admired so much also had sharp talons that could rip me to pieces.

So I spent the next ten years or so desperately trying to improve myself—to get better so that I didn't irritate or anger him. However, what I was really doing was dying inside and becoming a fake person who was unable to express any thoughts or opinions unless they were pleasing to him and coincided with his views. I was always tense and walking on eggshells, trying to avoid the inevitable punishment that would come if I displeased him. Our two children were trapped in the same cycle, knowing that Dad was the head of the home and everything had to revolve around his wishes.

Things went from bad to worse until eventually he assaulted my daughter so severely that the school took her to the police station to lay a charge. She was removed from our home and put in a Children's home for eight months. Throughout all of this, Jeff never thought he had done anything wrong, and he would continually blame everybody else for any trouble in his life, never acknowledging his part and the heartache he was causing. For my part, I was always desperately hoping and praying that things would change. I never wanted to leave him, as my marriage vows are sacred to me, and I thought that if only I could love him enough, he would change. I also felt very sorry for him, knowing that he had suffered many hurts in his life and that now he was continuing this cycle of hurting others.

However, I finally came to the realization that if I stayed with him, the only future I could see for myself would be insanity or suicide. Many times I came very close to both of those, but deep down inside I did not want either option, and I knew that somehow, somewhere I could have a better life. So I packed my bags and left him. My two teenage children were extremely relieved and gladly came with me. We moved to a small town about thirty-five miles away from the city where Jeff still lives.

At the time of writing, it's been just over one year since I left. It has been a difficult year in many ways, but also a very, very good year—a year of freedom and finding myself again, taking up hobbies and pursuits I had abandoned years ago, and learning how to live as a single person again, with two teenagers to care for. I could never have done it without the help and encouragement of family and friends who lovingly gathered around me when I was finally able to make the decision to leave. Before that, I had been so isolated, trying to make it on my own and not wanting anyone to really know how bad things were for fear that they would judge or condemn me. Instead, I have experienced only loving care beyond words.

Most of all, I have realized that there is actually nothing "wrong" with me. I am a dove and not an eagle, and I can be a very good and happy dove if I don't compare myself to the eagle and allow him to sink his talons into my body and soul. To all the "doves" who might be reading this, my encouragement to you is to spread your wings and *fly*. Be the best you can be and don't allow anyone to keep you trapped. If you are trapped and afraid, ask God to give you the courage to take that step of faith, knowing that you were not created to live in fear and misery. You were created to live a full, abundant life and be a blessing to others.

About the Author

Rosemary K. was born and raised on a farm in South Africa, the youngest of five children and the only daughter. At the age of twenty-five, she started traveling. She lived and worked on a ship for two years, circumnavigating South and Central America. It was on the ship that she met and married Jeff and attended Bible College. For the next eighteen years, she was involved with Mission work in various countries, finally returning to South Africa in 2003. Two beautiful children resulted from her marriage. She continues to live in South Africa, where she is now pursuing a career in writing, which has always been her passion.

Be Your Own Success Story

By Jack Thomas

"Life isn't about finding yourself. Life is about
creating yourself."
—George Bernard Shaw, Author

From Being Bullied to Being Successful

Bullying: one of the most hideous words in the English language.
Bullies have a fragile exterior shell and are often lacking interior
substance, for which they punish their victims. They are scared to
confront their own demons, yet "brave" enough to expose the
weaknesses in other people.

Every child goes through some form of bullying at various stages
of life, but bullying happens to adults, too. Unfortunately, it happens
in all walks of life and always will. Bullying will always exist in the
world, but it is up to us as individuals to not allow it to control our
world. If this story improves the life of one person, whether it helps a
victim or makes a bully realize the error of his or her ways, it will
have been worth writing.

I write this today as a competitive athlete, personal trainer, and
fitness model. I have achieved all of my dreams, and things are still
improving to this day through belief in myself, maturity, and personal
growth. I did it and so can you. I hope you enjoy my story.

Digging Up the Past

As a child I had spurts of popularity, yet being popular is often a fad like yoyos, pogs, football stickers, bangles, and Tamagotchi. Popularity comes and goes for a lot of people, whereas others seem to make it stick. Many people say popularity and bullying are both rites of passage, but I disagree—*learning* from them is the real rite of passage.

Children often spend their entire youth trying to please others and seeking social acceptance. This is often where bullying begins. When we are in the midst of our teen years, it is hard to understand, but then we grow into adulthood and the passage of time reveals the truth. That truth can be an ugly bearer of reality. Only how you feel about yourself matters in the long run.

Where Did It Begin?

I had significant insecurities growing up. In primary school, things were not so bad, but I spent months of each year in the hospital and was often very sick due to a serious lifelong medical condition. During the easier years, I didn't have to think about what I wanted from life and could just "be."

When I was eight years old, my mother formed a new relationship a few years after divorcing my biological father. This man, whom she later married, was abusive and used my medical problems to punish me. Those times were some of the most humiliating of my life, and they left psychological scars that are still healing.

The Body Can Heal a Lot Faster Than the Mind

It would take seventeen years for me to be able to tell anybody about the abuse, and my insecurities manifested as a result of those events. Some of those problems subsided over time but were replaced by others as I got to a stage where I wanted to pretend my medical condition did not exist.

I had plenty of friends and was popular during the first three years of secondary school—until puberty kicked in among my friends and I still had not begun to develop. I was five-and-a-half stone (seventy-seven pounds) and five feet five at the age of fifteen and looked a lot younger than I was. My health had gotten a lot worse, and I looked like death.

After summer break when we all returned to school, something had changed among a large group of my friends. The change was perpetrated by one student who was popular. He decided that I no longer needed to be part of his social circle, and slowly but surely he turned half the students against me. I quickly learned how shallow friendships can be and, to this day, I don't understand what I did wrong to those people. Yet I cannot dwell on these matters too much, as they would otherwise eat away at me.

Through Thick and Thin?

I first noticed fewer people speaking to me in the corridors. Someone always occupied my seat at the back of the school bus or in class. Dirty looks and sniggers seemed to come out of nowhere. I started to question what I'd done to deserve this treatment; the answer was usually nothing, which left me even more confused by the situation.

The open mocking then began—large groups of boys would

happily single me out on numerous occasions on the playing field, in class, or on the school bus. I was so weak and fragile that there was nothing I could really do to stop them. Bullying is all about intimidation, and these people fed on my weakness. Their treatment of me helped them mask their own insecurities and underlying problems.

The Method Behind the Madness

Most of us want to be accepted before we begin to accept ourselves growing up; we do it in reverse order. Bullies and their victims both seek acceptance but use different strategies to try and achieve it.

If bullies learned to confront their demons instead of seeking approval from others and living a life based on what others expect them to be, bullying would not exist. If victims had the confidence to not care or put up with what bullies did to them, bullying would be eliminated.

I always had friends—let me be clear about that. But situations changed drastically, and my friends were never there at the right times. I remember being pushed over and thrown to the floor a couple of times. I remember having cheese forcefully rubbed all over my face in front of an entire busload of pupils right outside my house. Verbal, physical, and mental bullying all happened at some point.

This and much more was all happening during the time when I was trying to deal with teen angst, do two hours of medication a day, fight off needing a double lung transplant, struggle with insomnia, and so much more. Daily.

A long list of events occurred, but it would take more than one chapter to mention them all. I ended up dreading going to school and found any reason to cut class. My schoolwork suffered as a result. In the aftermath of it all, I was left with bad memories, no self-esteem, bad grades, and incredibly poor health.

I had no drive to succeed, and everything slowly crumbled around me. It was horrible to be completely powerless against such odds—and the sad fact is that many people have suffered bullying much worse than I did.

Time to Man Up

After we all left school, my friends and I had the choice to stay on in college together. Luckily, I was placed in a class with all of my friends, and a large part of the bullying subsided dramatically. Even still, I became a dropout. In part because the bullying continued, I did not continue my education, and at times it can still be hard to give the bullies absolution. I was kicked out of both home and college, so I had to knuckle down, find a job, and make my own way in the world at the age of seventeen.

Ages eighteen and nineteen were very lackluster years for me, and I continued down a reckless path of no prospects. Fed up with being small and sick, I started bodybuilding and taking care of myself with medication and nutrition, and everything began to change.

However, it was not until I turned twenty-three that I began to finally understand what I wanted to do with my life. I started charity work and a website to help people with the same health condition as me, then became a competitive athlete as all my hard work in the gym started to pay off.

Rising Back Up

After I had sunk to the bottom, I realized that nobody else had the power to control me or my life. Not an illness, no bullies or naysayers—just me. I ended up guest speaking in schools, achieved sponsorship, and worked with television companies to make documentaries.

I believed I needed to make up for a great deal of lost time, so I gave everything I did one hundred percent. I am now working in the fitness industry helping athletes and supplement companies with promotions. I am a fitness model and physique athlete, I have broken records and competed at a national level, and I also work as a sports journalist.

Now that I am somewhat successful, it would be wrong to say I never think of what happened in the past. Those bullies—those people who used to make my life hell—all of them, especially the instigator of it all, I could now bully and intimidate.

The biggest triumph is those people getting to watch me make something of my life when they have not. The moment I truly realized how weak they were is when the power shifted over to me and I knew I could become the bully. As a man, I could never do that, even for revenge on the most deserving soul. The difference between a bully and a victim is strength, and it is always the bully who lacks it.

Some of those people even have the nerve to friend me on Facebook or try to say hello on the street, as though we were the best of buddies. Others cannot even look me in the eye out of cowardice. Here I am, now loving life, and you can, too.

Always know you can triumph.

About the Author

Jack Thomas is the pseudonym of a successful online entrepreneur based in the United Kingdom. His personal blog reaches over fifty thousand unique readers every month. He has worked in public relations, television, newspaper, and radio productions both in front of and behind the camera. In addition, he is a competitive fitness athlete and works as a signed model.

Apprehension

By Shiva

"Fear cuts deeper than swords."
—George R. R. Martin, Author *Game of Thrones*

I was eighteen years old. Although years have passed since then, my memory of the event is still crystal clear. Along with my group of friends, I was organizing a cricket tournament involving about thirty-five teams. As the key organizer, and since the event venue was close to my home, I used my grandpa's bicycle to commute. One day, a hefty guy named Damodar was trying to sit on the bicycle, which did not belong to him, and moreover he would have damaged it. Emotionally upset, I shouted at him to stay off the bike. He threatened me verbally and said that he would continue to sit on my bicycle no matter what. I felt helpless and screamed at him, all the while petrified that he could physically harm me. Some friends intervened to calm things down, but the guy continued to stare at me as he left the scene, shouting that he would take care of me later. I forgot about the incident, but Damodar did not. He was the neighborhood hoodlum and was given to vices of all kinds, including alcoholism, extortion, and bullying.

A couple of months later, while I was walking back from college, a hefty person accosted me and stopped me in my tracks. It took me some time to recognize him as Damodar, who was back with a vengeance. The cricket incident automatically played out in the back of my mind. I experienced a strange mixture of emotions: fear of physical threat and loss of face. He dragged me to a desolate side lane and said, "You were very strong, along with your friends, that day at the cricket ground. Now you are at my mercy." As I gathered my wits to handle the situation, my nerves failed me. I asked him to let me go, but he would not. He punched me repeatedly in my stomach and left me in pain. I managed to reach home but did not share my story with anyone.

Living in the same neighborhood, I would occasionally come across Damodar and freeze at the sight of him for the first couple of years. I felt a sense of apprehension that he could harm me again. I avoided crossing paths with him and would hide whenever I saw him from a distance. It was then that I started wondering why someone else's bullying behavior should affect my attitude toward life. I confided in some of my close friends, and we worked out a plan that we would hang out together. This gave me lot of mental fortitude and enabled me not to be psyched out by Damodar.

Later on, as I did well academically and played cricket for my university, Damodar became a distant memory. My community recognized me for my success, and I was seen as the role model in our residential community.

After completing my education, I joined the Indian army as a commissioned officer and underwent training in various physical and mental faculties. While on one of my vacations home, I found out that Damodar had passed away. His vices had gotten the better of him. I will be honest and say that I could not get Damodar out of my mind, even though the entire incident lasted barely two or three minutes. This minor incident seemed to have had an indelible impact on my subconscious; however, slowly but surely I have put it behind me like a bad dream.

My inclination toward academics and my interest in sports, which culminated in a career in the Indian army, prove what resolve can achieve.

It is not wrong to be afraid or to recall people or circumstances when we have been bullied. It would be useless, however, to dwell for long on such incidents. To move on and do meaningful things in life are more important. Certain things in our lives are within our control, and others are not. A prayer comes to mind: "God, give me the serenity to accept the things I cannot change, the courage to change the things I can, and the wisdom to know the difference."

About the Author

Shiva is based in Hyderabad, India. He enjoys writing human interest stories. He is actively associated with civil society activities with a focus on the environment.

Mean Girls

By Anonymous

"Everything is funny as long as it is happening
to somebody else."
—Will Rogers, Entertainer

Lauren was ugly on the inside, where it counts. Unfortunately, she was also beautiful on the outside, where it matters—in middle school. She was the girl with naturally crimped blond hair, giant blue eyes, and nice sneakers; thus, in the '90s, despite wearing glasses, she was automatically "cool." That's not to say she didn't work for it. She worked hard and fast to hitch onto the bandwagon of anyone else with popularity potential. The one she idolized the most was a girl named Diane, whom all the prepubescent boys loved because she looked even more like a Barbie doll.

In the grand scheme of things, I'm pretty sure it doesn't matter what you do and who you are at age twelve. But at the time, it seemed like a big deal to those who experienced the wrath of mean girls. While not the queen, Lauren was their war general. If Lauren didn't like you, you were an outcast. She would actively lobby against you with the enthusiasm of one who has nothing better to do with her life than wreak misery on others. She would find fault with you to no end just because that was her thing. I think it made her stand out, gave her an edge, made her a little more than the cling-on to Diane. If Lauren had read Machiavelli, she likely would have agreed with his philosophy that if one cannot be loved, it is better to be feared.

I know because I was subjected to her ridicule. In art class, one of the boys put up a deliberately lewd painting that resembled a male organ. Most girls wouldn't know what it was at such a young age—I hope—but rumors quickly spread that it was, in fact, what it was. A large outburst of snickering ensued. The teacher, being raised in more innocent times, did not make the connection. For some reason, Lauren took it upon herself to announce that no one was more likely to have created the painting than me. From there, the rumor spread that I was some kind of deviant. Lauren delighted in this opportunity to psychoanalyze all my actions. One time when I capped a pen more than once, Lauren shouted loudly to the entire classroom that this was perverse.

Our school had a swimming pool. My class had to learn how to float in case we ever fell into a river and had to save ourselves from drowning. I think there was a bit of paranoia in the '90s about freak accidents. Regardless, when all the girls went to swim for the first time, I (always prepared), thought ahead and brought a giant bottle of shampoo. None of the other girls had such foresight. One of my friends, Patty, asked to use some shampoo. Seeing Patty take the shampoo, a couple of other girls proceeded to take some shampoo as well. I guess they thought it was public shampoo or something—that was how huge the bottle was that I brought. Eventually, Lauren came into the shower room and took some shampoo as well. When I went to get some shampoo *from my own bottle*, Lauren announced loudly that I was stealing shampoo and was obviously a thief. Patty was quick to correct her. But Lauren still seemed hell-bent on attributing as many vices to me as she could. (The hero version of me would have ripped the shampoo right out of her hair.)

The rest of my middle school experience was characterized by other frequent attempts on Lauren's part to be relevant. She would often fail, but that didn't stop her from trying. For my part, I tried to ignore her because it was obvious to me that Lauren was desperate for attention of any kind. Ignoring her didn't stop her, though.

In my life, I have encountered a few crazy people, but Lauren from middle school tops my list. She was one of those people who went out of their way to be annoying for no reason. She made my youth stressful with incessant verbal attacks. Although I rarely think of her now, I hope she has turned into someone more substantial and that her childhood was not reflective of who she is today. It's not because I give a damn about her but rather because I think it would be awful to have more people like her in the world.

Lauren was the stereotypical mean girl—the kind that people laugh about in movies, whose behavior is so outrageous that it's hard to believe. The kind most people wish would get what they deserve. When you are young, it can be tough to cope when you are experiencing bullying. As a child, you don't necessarily have the social skills or resources to deal with whack jobs. I think that parents and authority figures have a responsibility to step in, but not every parent or authority figure acts responsibly. In life, there are a lot of passengers rather than drivers. People often don't take leadership roles or intervene when they should.

I was lucky in that I moved on from middle school to a high

school that Lauren did not attend and probably would have dropped out of. I never found out what happened to her, nor do I really care. In the best-case scenario, she evolved from being a horrible child to a more mature adult. In the worst-case scenario, she bred little monsters like herself who continue to terrorize innocent people. At any rate, what I have learned from my experience with Lauren is that there are nasty people in the world that others will invariably encounter. They can be unreasonable and even delusional. You can feel sorry for them, forgive them, and be a better person if you want. But really mean girls are forgotten 99 percent of the time once middle school has ended.

The best way to be remembered is by being a good person.

About the Author

Anonymous is a successful entrepreneur. She has competed in a variety of athletic events and believes that beauty comes from within and radiates outward.

Acknowledgments

We would like to thank all of the contributors to this compilation, who were brave enough to share their personal stories and kind enough to want to make a difference in the world by telling them. Bullying is a social evil and to be bullied often carries a social stigma. It is important that those who are being bullied realize they are not alone. Life can throw many challenges. When challenges are overcome, they can lead to wild success.

Thank you to all those who have supported this book and this work through reviews and word of mouth. If you found benefit from this volume, please do share this with others. We would love to hear from you on your thoughts. You can visit us at ReadingHarbor.com.

Printed in Great Britain
by Amazon